Robin Hood – The Real Story

The myth creators have dominated the Robin Legend for too long. It is now time for the real story to be told.

The only book about Robin Hood that gives a complete life story of all the main characters based on the public records.

Brian Benison

Revised Edition

Published by Leslie Brian Benison   January 2008
Forest Town   Mansfield   Nottingham

Printed and bound in Great Britain by

IMPRINT PRINT AND DESIGN
CHURCH STREET
MANSFIELD   NOTTS.

IBSN   9780954847302

CONTENTS

Reigns of Kings of England

HENRY11	Reigned	1154-1189
RICHARD 1	Reigned	1189-1199
JOHN	Reigned	1199-1216
HENRY 111	Reigned	1216-1272
EDWARD 1	Reigned	1272-1307
EDWARD 11	Reigned	1307-1327

Chapter One

Background to the legend

For the past 700 years Robin Hood has been one of the most popular and well-remembered heroes of his country.

You only have to mention his name in most parts of the world and people will talk about the English outlaw who robbed from the rich and gave to the poor.

Robin is just as popular today as he has ever been, and his adventures as an outlaw have been the subject of many books, films and television programmes.

He has been portrayed by such great actors as Douglas Fairbanks, Errol Flynn, Richard Todd, and Richard Greene, amongst many others, and more recently by Kevin Costner. We also have a new television series made by the BBC.

Yet, despite all that has been said and written about his life, there is still a mystery about him.

Did he really exist?

It is not surprising that this question is often asked because the modern version of the legend, particularly the one used in films, doesn't bear any resemblance to the original tale.

We can forgive the filmmakers and storytellers for using poetic licence to exaggerate and add romance to the tales. Their role after all is to entertain and amuse their audience.

The never-ending distortion of the legend however, has led to the life of the real outlaw being gradually forgotten and replaced by that of a mythical figure. It is sad, because the real story is just as exciting and full of adventure as the fictitious one, if not even more so.

Anyone who has watched and enjoyed the many films about Robin Hood's life would naturally assume that Robin Hood was an outlaw during the 12th century reign of King Richard the Lionheart. It is a magical story of a dashing and swashbuckling hero defending the crown of England whilst the King, Richard the Lionheart, was away from the country fighting in the religious crusade wars.

Robin and his followers were outlawed for defying the attempts of the Sheriff of Nottingham and the King's brother prince John, to take over control of the country and impose heavy taxes on the poor. The outlaws were forced to live in Sherwood Forest on the proceeds of robbery, and feeding on the King's deer, whilst fighting injustice and defying all the attempts of the Sheriff to capture them.

When King Richard returned to England he thanked and pardoned the outlaws, allowed Robin to marry his lovely Maid Marian, and everybody lived happily thereafter.

It makes a great film but there is no truth whatsoever in this interpretation of the legend. It is nothing more than a fanciful tale. So where did it all go wrong.

For more than two hundred years following the death of Robin Hood the ballad composers and historians of the day were in no doubt that he was a real person and an outlaw in the second half of the 13th century. This was during the reigns of King Henry III and his son, Edward I.

Then, during the 16th century, and at the height of Robin Hood's national fame, the writers and historians decided to make dramatic changes to the legend without any proof to support their theories.

The fact that Robin Hood became an outlaw because of his fight for the parliamentary system of government that we take so much for granted these days, was quite simply forgotten.

The 16th century saw the beginning of the myth that the lifetime of our outlaws was during the reign of King Richard the Lionheart. His social status was changed too, from a landowning farmer to a disinherited Earl of Huntingdon no less.

A strange claim as Robin wa s known as a great archer, a trademark of the yeoman class. A 14th century quotation at the time of the poet Chaucer said that 'A yeoman and his bow are inseparable'.

The nobility on the other hand, were trained in the art of jousting and the use of the lance.

The ancient ballads also refer to Robin Hood as being a yeoman. The most famous and reliable ballad is the one known as the 'The Lytell Geste', which is acknowledged as being the foundation of the Robin Hood legend. It is also the most important source of information about his outlaw life which can be verified by the public records.

The ballad begins with an introduction by the storyteller.

> 'Come listen to me gentlemen'
> 'That be of freeborn blood'
> 'I shall tell you of a good yeoman'
> 'His name is Robin Hood'

The dictionary definition of a yeoman does vary. It can be an attendant of a member of the nobility, but the historical version is that of a freehold landowner who farms his own land, a fitting description of our real outlaw.

Richard the Lionheart and Prince John

Although the reign of King Richard the Lionheart during the years 1189-1199 is far too early for the real Robin Hood, it is possible to see how this myth could have developed.

Richard's younger brother John once had the custody of Nottingham castle and a hunting lodge in Sherwood Forest. This was at Clipstone Park near Mansfield which Richard did visit on his return from the crusade wars. This was in fact before Robin Hood had been born.

The town of Mansfield is acknowledged as being at the heart of Sherwood Forest, and which was in the following century, to become closely associated with the real Robin Hood and his fellow outlaws.

At the time of Shakes peare the poet Michael Drayton, and playwrights Munday and Chettle, described Mansfield as being one of the main bases of the outlaws.

King Richard who is always described as the Lionheart because of his bravery, succeeded his father Henry II as King of England in 1189, but only spent a few months of his ten-year reign in England. The rest of the time was either spent fighting in the Crusade wars, or living in France.

Although born in England, Richard regarded France as his real home, only speaking in his native tongue of French. He actually did little for England, using the country's wealth and taxing the people heavily to raise money for his crusade. He is reported to have said that 'he would willingly sell London if he could find a buyer.'

When he left England for the crusades, Richard snubbed his brother John by appointing as regents with the power to rule the country in his absence, Hugh Pudsey the Bishop of Durham, and Richard's Chancellor William Longchamp.

It did prove a wise decision because John was indeed disloyal and treacherous to his brother by undermining King Richard's authority and trying to claim the English throne.

On his way to the holy lands Richard was successful in taking both Cyprus and Acre, but failed to defeat the army of the Muslim leader Saladin, and retake Jerusalem for the Christian faith.

Back at home in England however, things got so bad for Richard because of John's scheming that he was warned to return home soon, or have no kingdom to come home to.

Richard negotiated a peace treaty with Saladin but on his way home his ship was shipwrecked, leaving him with no choice but to travel by land in Europe. Because of his unpopularity he travelled in the disguise of a pilgrim with a long flowing beard but was recognised in Austria and held as a prisoner. He was then transferred to Germany with a large ransom demand for his release.

The English people were heavily taxed again to pay for Richard's release with gold and silver treasures being taken from the churches and Abbeys to pay towards the ransom.

When the ransom was eventually paid, Richard returned to England. Although welcomed home in London, he had to travel throughout the land to restore his authority.

Surprisingly he met unexpected resistance at Nottingham when the keepers of the castle refused to hand over control and even after burning down the outer gates, Richard still couldn't gain access to the castle. The terms of surrender were finally agreed but only after the arrival of the army of Richard's old friend Hugh Pudsey, the Bishop of Durham.

During his brief stay in Nottingham, Richard spent a day hunting from John's hunting lodge at Clipstone Park, and said how pleased he was with Sherwood Forest and the day's sport.

The visit is well documented and shows quite clearly that whilst in Sherwood, King Richard did not meet or pardon any outlaws.

Whilst out hunting in Sherwood Forest for deer and wild boar however, there was an incident with a stag known as 'The Hart Royale'. Richard chased a large hart which managed to escape by leaping over the wooden perimeter fence surrounding the Park.

MEETING OF RICHARD AND BISHOP PUDSEY.

Richard issued a proclamation that no person should kill or molest the hart so that it could return to the safety of the royal hunting Park.

The hart was said to have escaped to Barnsdale, the old English name for the district now known as Bassetlaw in the north of Nottinghamshire. The area was in the following century to be co-incidentally, the home of Robin Hood and his fellow outlaws.

The false theories linking Robin Hood to the reign of King Richard the Lionheart however didn't just fade away but were given a new lease of life following the publication of the fictitious adventure book 'Ivanhoe'. It was written by the author Sir Walter Scott, a distinguished novelist and poet who lived during the years 1771-1832.

Ivanhoe was a romantic ta le of a Saxon knight returning to England from the crusade wars and seeking to regain his inheritance which had been denied him. The book created the impression that there was a bitter hatred between the Saxons and the Normans, when in fact the two races were beginning to live in harmony. Robin Hood was a character introduced into the fanciful tale as the mythical Robert of Locksley who helped Ivanhoe regain justice for the Saxons. This was done in support of King Richard the Lionheart against Prince John and his officials.

Sir Walter Scott placed some real facts into the story to make it appear authentic, such as the holding of Richard as a prisoner in Europe, and the collection of a large ransom for his release. It also told of John's attempts to claim the English throne and King Richard's visit to the area.

The book's popularity further shaped the modern thinking of Robin Hood being an outlaw in the reign of King Richard the Lionheart. Scott must have been well aware however, of the ancient ballads on which the Robin Hood legend is based, which made it quite clear that the King of England at the time of Robin Hood was an Edward.

When was Robin Hood an outlaw?

Throughout history there had always been robbers, petty thieves and small family based groupings, but rarely such an outlaw as Robin Hood with a hundred or more followers.

The ancient historians who live closest to Robin Hood's lifetime, and the public records of the time, all support the view that he became an outlaw in the year 1265, following the defeat of Simon de Montfort at the battle of Evesham.

An examination of the public records of Sherwood Forest and the East Midland regions of England confirm only one occasion when there was such considerable outlaw activity of the type we associate with Robin Hood. This was during the years of 1265 to 1272.

The authorities expressed their concern about the many robberies being carried out by a large gathering of outlaws under their leader and master.

It was said that no religious person or travelling merchant was safe to travel, particularly in Sherwood Forest, without running the risk of being stopped and robbed by outlaws marauding on foot and on horseback both by day and night.

There were numerous occasions when the outlaws were easily able to defeat the troops sent out from Nottingham to capture them, the royal troops being humiliated and forced to travel back to Nottingham without their horses.

The authorities had to admit that the only way they could defeat the outlaws would be to find brave and courageous men willing enough to stand up to the outlaws.

It was also the time when a Sheriff of Nottingham was closely involved, and troubled, by an unusual and fearsome group of outlaws.

This Sheriff was Reginald de Grey who knew Robin Hood well from their days working together at Nottingham castle. Reginald became Sheriff in the year 1264, and Robin Hood an outlaw from the year 1265.

Whilst Reginald was Sheriff they are known to have gone hunting together in Sherwood Forest, particularly in the royal hunting Park of Bestwood, where they quite prepared to bend the forest laws. This was of course before they went their separate ways, and Robin became one of the most famous outlaws of all time.

The Sheriff of Nottingham is always regarded as being the villain of the tale, but Reginald was only doing his duty. He was actually a man the East Midland counties should be proud of, one of the youngest ever Sheriff's who became a great Parliamentarian and military leader for his country.

The earliest and most ancient historians to write about Robin Hood, and who told of the political crisis in England which caused this outlaw activity, were surprisingly not English but from England's neighbouring country, Scotland.

We had John Fordun, a pr iest from Aberdeen Cathedral and Walter Bower, the Abbot of Incholm, an island in the Firth of Forth near Edinburgh.

It is not too clear when John Fordun was actually born but is generally accepted as being around the year 1300. He dedicated his life to historical research, and is said to have wandered around the country like a curious bee in his quest for historical knowledge, by visiting various Abbeys, Colleges and Universities for the information he required.

Bower, who was born later in the 14 th century, continued and added to Fordun's work. Fordun covered the period from 1153 until his death in the year 1385 and came across the existence of England's most famous outlaw because of Scotland's involvement in English history.

During the civil wars that took place in England between King Henry III and his Barons in the years 1264 and 1265, the King of Scotland was asked by Henry to provide assistance with a large fighting force to help Henry defeat the rebellion against his rule led by Simon De Montfort.

Fordun said that following the defeat of Simon De Montfort at the battle of Evesham in the year 1265, there arose from the banished and those people dispossessed of their land and property that most famous outlaw Robin Hood together with Little John and their companions.

Fordun and Bower commented on how the people took great pleasure in hearing of the outlaws many exploits from jesters, storytellers and minstrels. They were fascinated by the outlaws many feats of daring and disregard of the law.

We have to remember t hat during this particular period there was still a dominating French influence over England as a result of the French Norman invasion two centuries earlier. William the Conqueror defeated the Anglo Saxons at the battle of Hastings. The successful Normans seized control of England and were now the ruling class.

The 13th century however, saw demands for change and for restrictions on the absolute power of the King. There was a strong desire for the native born Englishmen to have a far greater say in the running of their own country, rather than the favoured foreigners of King Henry III.

Henry, the son of King John, was the King of England during the years of 1216 and 1272, and married Eleanor of Provence, a region in the south of France. Her foreign connections are said to have dominated the court.

Matthew Paris a St. Albans monk and historian during part of King Henry's reign provided an interesting insight into the conditions prevailing in England at this time. Paris expressed frustration and anger at Henry's persistent fault of appointing his relatives and foreigners to positions of authority in both the Church and the country.

It was King Henry's agreem ent to change, and then his subsequent failure to carry out these reforms, that led to armed conflict with his Barons, and the emergence of Robin Hood as an outlaw.

A national hero.

During Robin Hood's lifetime very few people were able to read or write. They did not have the benefit of the instant means of communication that we enjoy today such as the Internet, radio, television, newspapers and news bulletins.

For the majority of the people the only way to keep in touch with current affairs and events was by word of mouth. Their main source of information and knowledge came from easy to remember poems and songs told by the storytellers of the day. They told in rhyme and verse the deeds of the great heroes and events of the past. These songs and poems became known as ballads and those concerning Robin Hood were to become amongst the most popular of all the ancient ballads.

As the many stories of Robin Hood's outlaw life spread throughout the country, he developed from a local figure to a national hero.

Despite his death in t he year 1293, Robin's fame and popularity lived on, and an annual festival came to be held in his honour. It became known as the May games taking place on the first of May.

The origin of the games and festival was primarily to encourage the practice of archery, of which Robin Hood was considered to be the master. Skilled archers were important, of course, for the defence of the country, and in times of war.

This annual festival proved to be very popular with the people, and came to be treated as a public holiday. Nearly everyone stopped what they were doing for the day in order to take part in the festivities.

The people came together in their own communities to not only watch the archery contests and enjoy the festivities but to pay homage to the memory of Robin Hood.

Lysons, in his 'Environs of London', gave the accounts of the churchwardens of Kingston upon Thames listing the expenditure of money for the May games which took place that year. This list included money for the dresses and ornaments plus wages for the Morris Dancers and actors who performed as Robin Hood and Maid Marion. The stage plays and lighting of bonfires were held in the evening.

The holding of these festivities however, was not too well received by certain members of the establishment, and there were many unsuccessful attempts to ban them.

Certain members of the clergy were not happy about the holding and popularity of the festival. They felt that the people were more interested in attending the festival and celebrating Robin Hood, rather than going to church.

An example of this is in the mid 16th century, in one of the sermons of Bishop Latimer to King Edward VI.

The Bishop complained that on travelling home-ward from London he sent word ahead that he would preach there in the morning, as it was a Sunday, a holy day.

On his arrival at the church the following day, the Bishop found the doors of the church were locked. After waiting for a while he was told that this was Robin Hood's day and the people would be unable to attend church. We quote from part of the sermon where the audience must have laughed.

'It is no laughing matter my friends, but a weeping matter. A heavy matter that under the pretence of gathering for Robin Hood, a traitor and a thief, they put out the preacher and had his office less esteemed, with the people preferring Robin Hood before the ministration of God's word.'

The people however, were very reluctant to give up their annual celebrations despite the opposition from the clergy and certain magistrates.

In Edinburgh, for example, in the year of 1561, there were riots on the streets when the local magistrate tried to stop the people holding the festival.

There was a surprising royal interest in our outlaw however, King Henry VIII, famous for his six wives, was particularly fascinated by the legend and loved to take part in the annual celebrations and May Games.

We are told by Hall in hi s Chronicle of an incident that took place shortly after Henry VIII's coronation, and whilst he was at Westminster with his new Queen. King Henry, in company with the Earls of Wiltshire and Essex and other noblemen surprised the Queen one morning by coming into her chamber dressed in short coats, and with hoods over their heads. They carried swords and bows and arrows and after imitating Robin Hood's men for the amusement of the Queen, they left the Queen's chamber.

On another occasion both Henry VIII and his Queen, in company with many Lords and Ladies, travelled onto the high ground on Shooter's Hill to watch the archers from the King's guard practising their archery skills. The archers were dressed for the occasion in medieval costumes, in the style of the clothes that had been worn by Robin Hood and his men of old.

When the archery exhibition ended, the King and Queen were escorted into the forest and served with venison and wine whilst being entertained by the King's men.

This was an attempt to re-create how it was believed that Robin Hood and his men lived in the forest It also shows how well known the Lytell Geste ballad must have been. This performance fits the description in the ballad of Robin Hood's unique method of robbery where the victims were treated as guests and invited to dine with the outlaws. Once the meal was over, however, they were made to pay well for their food and entertainment.

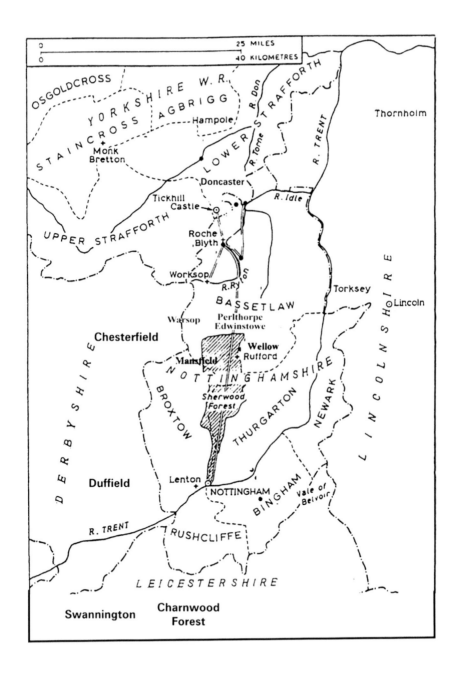

Why Sherwood Forest?

Tradition and the involvement of the Sheriff of Nottingham tell us that Sherwood Forest was the main base for Robin Hood and his fellow outlaws.

There is an ancient poem written on manuscript paper which was found in Lincoln Cathedral. It is dated around the year 1400 and contains the following words.

'Robin Hood in Sherwood stood'.

Sherwood was classified as a royal forest and extended for some twenty miles, 30 kilometres north of Nottingham, with certain areas set aside as royal hunting parks. These were surrounded by high wooden perimeter fences designed to keep the livestock in, and the general public out.

Only certain members of the ruling class were allowed to hunt in Sherwood and foresters were employed to carry out the strict forest laws.

The forest rules clearly st ated that 'be it only lawful for Bishops, Earls and Barons to take one or two deer, and if no forester be present, then a horn must be sounded'.

The foresters however were well known for turning a blind eye to certain offenders, and were quoted at the time as 'not always doing what they aught'.

There were however, certain areas set aside for use by the common folk where they could take wood and graze their livestock, although these were limited

Sherwood was under the dire ct control of the Sheriff, and whilst Reginald de Grey was Sheriff, he used Nottingham castle as his home.

Reginald's duties spread beyond Nottingham to the East Midland counties of Nottingham, Derby and Leicester, with his official title being that of the Sheriff of Nottingham and Derby.

The main theme of the Robin Hood legend is of course, the conflict between the outlaws and the Sheriff of Nottingham. One of the main reasons for Robin and his fellow outlaws being so closely associated with this area was that three of the leaders of the Barons revolt against King Henry III's rule, came from here.

The Barons leader was Simon De Montfort, the Earl of Leicester. His chief supporters were Robert Ferrers the Earl of Derby and Henry Hastings whose family had connections with the Manor of Mansfield in Sherwood Forest.

Our famous outlaw was at differing times, to serve under these three leaders.

Following Simon De Montfort's death on the battlefield at Evesham, the capture of Robert Ferrers at Chesterfield, and the premature death of Henry Hastings, the outlaws had to regroup. Their new leader was Robin Hood.

It was not too surprising, therefore, that they would seek sanctuary in this east midland region where they could expect to find help and support particularly in the Manor of Mansfield and the northern part of Sherwood Forest.

Robin and his fellow outla ws were able to receive help from detection and arrest from a local knight Richard Foliot. He had a castle home in Wellow on the north-eastern edge of Sherwood Forest, described in the geste ballad as being 'double ditched and walled off from the road'.

Although the castle is no longer in existence, the double ditch can still be seen. There is a note in the public records of Richard Foliot, at the time of Robin Hood, applying for and receiving planning permission to build this double ditch. No other castle in the area has such a distinctive feature.

Sir Richard Foliot remained neutral during the conflict between King Henry and Simon De Montfort, although he was a sympathiser of De Montfort's cause, and once acted as a temporary Sheriff of Nottingham during De Montfort's brief rule of England.

During Robin Hood's lifetime Nottinghamshire was divided into six self-ruling regions, the largest of which was in the northern part of the county and included part of Sherwood Forest in its boundary. The district is identified today as the district of Bassetlaw, and sign posted for visitors as Robin Hood country.

At the time of the Domesday Book, written following the Norman French conquest of England, the Book listed the land and property in England. The district of Bassetlaw was interpreted into Latin by the court scribes as Bernesdelau.

Over the years it changed to Bersetlau before settling into its more modern form of Bassetlaw.

Robin and his men were able to settle here because local landowners in the district, who had supported Simon de Montfort, were to provide land bases for the outlaws.

Fordun and Bower told of an incident concerning Robin Hood and the Sheriff in this particular district.

Although as clerics they strongly disapproved of Robin Hood's lifestyle as a robber and a thief, they did admire his religious devoutness.

They remarked on how Robin never lost his religious faith, and loved to hear mass whenever he could. This was limited of course, whilst he was an outlaw.

They described one occasion he was tracked down by a certain Sheriff and his officers. When Robin's fellow outlaws saw the Sheriff approaching they warned their leader of the danger, and begged him to leave the service before the Sheriff arrived. Robin refused to interrupt the service and carried on praying.

After the service was over he fought off the Sheriff's men and made his escape. It was said that Robin believed in an old religious saying.

'God will always help the man who often hears mass.'

Who is the real Robin Hood?

One of the main reasons for the confusion in the legend is that Robin Hood is not the real name of our famous outlaw, but an affectionate nickname given to him by the people.

Throughout history there has always been a tendency for certain people to attract a nickname that remains forever in the minds of the people, rather than the real and proper name of the individual concerned.

A modern example is the American outlaw known as Billy the Kid. He acquired this nickname because of his youth. The mention of his real name, William Bonny however, will not attract much attention but the name Billy the Kid will bring an immediate response and recognition.

The outlaw life of both Robin Hood and Billy the Kid have something in common in that they were both pursued and brought down by a Sheriff who was once their friend.

When Robin Hood lived his life as an outlaw, he would of course, have been very eager to keep his identity a secret.

Had he been successful we would never have known his real name. But we know he received a pardon, and became known to the Sheriff of Nottingham.

His receiving of a pardon would have been required by law to be noted in the public records under his real name.

So what is the name of the outlaw who became known as Robin Hood?

Who is the most notable En glish outlaw of all time who made Sherwood Forest one of the most famous, and well-known forests throughout the world?

And who is the outlaw wh o made his enemy, the Sheriff of Nottingham, as famous as himself?

Thanks to the historians John Fordun and Walter Bower, who covered the period of Robin Hood's lifetime, we know when, why, and where he was an outlaw.

They said that following the defeat of Simon de Montfort at the battle of Evesham in the year 1265, his supporters were disinherited and forced to live as outlaws.

The public records reveal outlaw activity on a large and unprecedented scale during this period. The outlaws ruled the forest areas and the authorities feared that Nottingham castle was in danger of being overrun by the outlaws.

There is only one leader of a large number of outlaws of which this could be said, and that is a man known as Roger Godberd.

From the year 1265, Roger Godberd and his men had to move throughout the East Midland area, avoiding capture and defeating the troops sent out to capture them.

Their various bases were at Chesterfield and Duffield in the county of Derby and Charnwood forest in Leicestershire before they finally settled in Sherwood Forest. It was here that they stayed for just over four years until the winter of the years 1271-72, defying the Sheriff and the Nottingham authorities at will.

In the history of Sh erwood Forest and Nottingham there has never been such a large gathering of outlaws, either before or since Roger Godberd and his men.

For further confirmation that Roger Godberd must have been the man who was given the nickname of Robin Hood we turn to the ancient ballads.

The ballad, which is acknowledged as the foundation of the Robin Hood legend, is the ballad known as the Lytell Geste. It gives a life-story of Robin and his fellow outlaws and of the other main characters in the legend.

The ballad makes it quite clear that apart from Robin Hood and the Sheriff of Nottingham, there is a third main character in the legend, a knight known as Sir Richard.

He is a knight who gave help and protection to Robin and his fellow outlaws to avoid detection, and arrest by the Sheriff of Nottingham.

The Geste ballad is not aware of the real names of the three main characters, calling the Sheriff only by the name of his office, and the knight Sir Richard.

By linking the geste ballad to the public records however we can establish that the Sheriff of Nottingham in the tale was a Reginald de Grey, and that the third main character was the knight Sir Richard Foliot.

All the evidence therefore, points to the fact that the man known as Robin Hood must be Roger Godberd. He was the leader of the outlaws during this period of time, and until the final showdown with the Sheriff, Reginald de Grey.

Godberd's life as an outlaw certainly mirrors the life of Robin Hood as told by the ballads.

So what is it that links these three main characters to the legend and to the geste ballad in particular?

The geste ballad describes the castle of the knight Sir Richard as being surrounded by a double ditch, and walled off from the road.

In real life and the geste ballad, the knight Richard Foliot befriended Robin and his fellow outlaws, and gave them protection from arrest by the Sheriff of Nottingham.

The ballad confirmed by the public records, also tells of arrangements being made by the Sheriff to arrest the knight Sir Richard for helping the outlaws. At a hearing the knight, Richard Foliot received a pardon.

There is no doubting that Reginald de Grey is the Sheriff of the ballad. In the ballad the King instructed the Sheriff to recruit the finest archers in the land to capture the outlaws.

This is what Reginald de Grey did, with the counties of Nottingham, Derby and Leicester sharing the cost of this formidable army to finally defeat the outlaws.

In the Geste ballad Robin Hood was in the service of the crown for fifteen months, and lived for 22 years when his outlaw days were over. So did Roger Godberd.

Despite the over whelming evidence as to the identity of the real Robin Hood, it has not stopped other people being suggested as the real outlaw. One suggestion which is the most popular and strangest of them all is that by a Joseph Hunter from Wakefield in Yorkshire.

In a publication in the year of 1852, under the title 'The Ballad's Hero, Robin Hood' Hunter was to claim that Robin Hood was a 14th century outlaw from Wakefield.

This claim does seem very bizarre because according to his theory our famous outlaw would have been alive and active during the lifetime of the historian John Fordun. In his investigation Fordun had made it quite clear that Robin Hood was an outlaw in the previous century to himself.

Hunter took his lead from the theory of the 16th century writer John Leland who was the first person to ever suggest that Robin Hood could have had links to this area.

From a search of the Wakefield Manor Rolls Hunter found the name of a Robert Hode registered under the year 1317. On finding a Robyn Hood employed as a valet in the household accounts of King Edward II, he assumed the two men were the same person, and the real Robin Hood.

Hunter then linked the visit of Edward II to Yorkshire in 1323, and claimed that the King had met and pardoned this Wakefield Robert Hode, and took him into his service.

It is odd that anyone would think that the greatest archer in the land would be employed by the King as a valet cum servant. The two men were in fact different people, the valet being old and close to retirement. There is also no evidence to suggest that the King had pardoned any outlaw on this visit, or that the Wakefield Robert Hode had ever been the leader of any outlaws, or involved in any conflict with a Sheriff of Nottingham.

It does appear that both men have been dragged from obscurity, merely to try and justify a false theory.

The other claimants to Robin Hood all fail the same test in that their lives do not match the events of the Geste ballad, the cornerstone of the legend, have any support from the public records, or any link to a Sheriff of Nottingham.

The numerous myths and theorising about the legend show what a popular figure Robin Hood has become. At the end of the day however there is only one Robin Hood and that man is Roger Godberd.

No other outlaw before or since, has been able to give the authorities such a run-around as he was able to do, or defeat on so many occasions, the troops sent out to try and capture him.

Chapter Two

Life before becoming an Outlaw

In order to fully understand the reason for Roger Godberd becoming an outlaw, we need to start our story in the year 1258. King Henry III had made an agreement with his Barons, known as the Provisions of Oxford, offering a more democratic form of government for the English people.

It was however, the King's failure to keep his side of the agreement and the political turmoil that followed, which was to lead Roger, seven years later, into his life as one of the most famous outlaws of his country.

Roger Godberd, as a freehold landowning farmer would have remembered the year of 1258 very well. It was a year of unusually bad weather and harvests, which led to food shortages throughout the land, and some people to die of starvation.

The Godberd's were of the Anglo Saxon race who lived in Nottingham during the late 12th century. Roger and his family settled in the village of Swannington, twenty-five miles [40 kilometres] south of Nottingham, in Nottingham's neighbouring county of Leicester.

He was the largest landowner in the area and as such known as the village squire. He divided his land holdings into three sections described as Ridings, with a portion of his land being leased to the nearby Abbey of St. Mary's at Garendon. The Abbey and its convent were of the religious order of the Cistercians, and had been built in the year 1133. The lay brothers farmed the land in order to provide fresh food for its occupants.

This land was in later years, to be the cause of a bitter dispute between Roger and the Abbot of the Abbey, as Roger tried unsuccessfully to recover his land.

HENRY III.

Before his outlaw days began Roger had showed that he was not a man to be messed about with, and that he was quite prepared to take the law into his own hands.

In a land dispute with a Jordan Fleming which appears to be over money, Jordan claimed that Roger had robbed, and then ejected him from land in Swannington which he was leasing from Roger.

Roger chose to ignore Fleming's plea to the courts that he held a lease to the land, granted to him by Roger. The court had to finally order the Sheriff to threaten Roger that unless he came to the court and answered the charge, they would take his land and chattels.

Although there was no register of births, marriages and deaths until the 16th century, we can place Roger's birth as being around the year 1220.

This is because of an entry in the Fine Rolls of the year 1258, which noted his appearance in a local court to pay a fine on behalf of his young daughter, Diva.

Roger Godberd must have been particularly proud of his daughter because the name of Diva was derived from the ancient term for a goddess. We also know that he had a son named after him.

In a post mortem on Roger's death in the year 1293 his son Roger inherited his land and property, but had to fight off a challenge for the right to be known as the village squire.

We know that Roger had at least two brothers, one being Geoffrey, who was employed with him at Nottingham castle. The other was a younger brother William, who was in later years to join the outlaws.

Up to the present day the public records do not reveal the name of Roger's wife. As Roger is known throughout the world by his nickname of Robin Hood, so has his wife acquired the affectionate name of Maid Marian.

Until the year 1258, King Henry III had ruled England with absolute power and as a virtual dictator, without any regard to his English subjects.

A rebellion against his rule however led by Simon de Montfort, the Earl of Leicester, forced Henry into making concessions in the administration of the country and for the banishment of foreigners from England, particularly the King's greedy relatives.

Henry signed an agreement known as the Provisions of Oxford, in which a schedule of grievances was drawn up and a council of 24 members elected, 12 chosen by the King, and 12 by the Barons. Their task was to carry out reforms in both the Church and the country.

The Barons also negotiated a peace treaty with France in which they surrendered the English claims to Normandy, Maine and Anjou, thus breaking the old ties to France.

Over the following years Roger Godberd must have noticed the changes taking place throughout England.

For the first time the people were having a say in the running of their own country. There were new procedures and bodies in place to deal with the grievances of the people, and to put right any injustices that had occurred.

A few years later King Henry III decided to change his mind, and to consider the Provisions of Oxford agreement as not being legally binding.

Peter Savoy, an Italian nobleman who was related to Henry's wife Queen Eleanor, was a prominent member of those people who encouraged the King to break his oath to the Provisions. This was despite the fact he had supported the Barons when the agreement was made in 1258.

Savoy was a typical example of the way foreigners were favoured by King Henry. He was knighted by the King, given possession of some large estates, and the title of the Earl of Richmond.

Savoy made plans for a jousting tournament to be held at Northampton, but the King intervened to stop it taking place. He feared the English knights would easily defeat his favoured foreigners.

Peter caused quite a stir in England by bringing several foreign ladies over to England for the purpose of getting them married to some of the English nobles.

His association with Nottingham and the East Midlands came when he acquired Tickhill castle, on Nottingham's northern border, and arranged for one of his foreign ladies to marry Edmund de Lacy, the Earl of Lincoln.

In the July of the year 1262, Savoy caused outrage in the country when it became known that Richard de Clare, the Earl of Gloucester, and a leading member of the Barons party, had been found dead by poisoning at Savoy's home. This was after accepting an invitation to dine there.

Fearing both retribution, and the growing hostility of the English towards all foreigners, Savoy decided to leave the country forever.

During this period of time and change we had the entry into public life of Robert Ferrers, the Earl of Derby, and Henry Hastings. Both men were to be closely involved with Roger Godberd when he became an outlaw.

The two members of the nobility were born at a similar time, and lost their fathers at an early age. As they were both unable to claim their inheritance until they reached the age of 21 years, they became wards of the King who made arrangements for the custody of their lands.

The control and ward ship of a person's estates could be very profitable, and the King was often found guilty of favouring his family and foreign relatives.

Robert Ferrers, who was born in the year 1239, was to feel particularly aggrieved in the way his inheritance was handled by the King.

At the age of nine, he was forced into an arranged marriage with a relative of the King, and in the year 1257, the Queen and Peter Savoy, paid an enormous sum to the King for the custody of Ferrers estate, showing how valuable the control of a person's land could be.

In the year 1260 Robert Ferrers, the Earl of Derby, was eventually able to gain control of his land. Although he paid homage to the crown, he never lost his distrust of the King and his favoured foreigners.

It is not too surprising, therefore, that the young Earl chose to enter public life as one of the main supporters of the Baronial cause, and democratic reform of the country.

Henry Hastings, who was four years older than Robert Ferrers, was to fare much better in his ward ship following the death of his father in the year 1250.

The historian Matthew Paris, described Henry's father as a distinguished knight, and a wealthy Baron. His mother Ada was the daughter of David, the Earl of Huntingdon, and brother of the King of Scotland, giving Henry a connection to the Scottish throne, and title of the Earl of Huntingdon. In later years his son was to lay claim to this title.

The Hastings's family association with Sherwood Forest occurred in the year 1238 when Henry's father was given the Manor of Mansfield in Sherwood Forest. On the death of his father in the July of 1250, the King granted the ward ship of Henry's estates to a Geoffrey de Lusignan. The following year he transferred it to William de Cantelupe a close friend of Simon de Montfort.

This choice of guardian proved to be very fortunate for young Henry, as he fell in love with and married Joan, his guardian's daughter. From this happy marriage, they had two sons and three daughters.

Henry served his King well, and in the year 1260 he was called to arms to help defeat an army from Wales.

The King decided to ignore his agreement to the Provisions of Oxford and further infuriated his Barons by persuading the Pope to release him from his oath to the Provisions.

In the inevitable struggle for power that followed, Prince Edward was to play a more dominating role in the affairs of the country. As the eldest son of King Henry, Edward was of course the heir to the English throne.

The King greeted his birth at Westminster with a great sigh of relief, because it was thought that the Queen would never be able to have a child. To celebrate, King Henry requested that all the gifts should only be of the best and of great value. This prompted a wit of the day to comment that 'God gave us this infant, but our Lord King sells him to us.'

Edward was given the Earldom of Chester an important trading port and prosperous town, which was the gateway to Wales and of great military value. Chester was important too for Reginald de Grey our Sheriff of Nottingham. He was a childhood friend of Prince Edward, and was in later years to be appointed as Edward's Chief Justice of Chester.

Edward became familiar with Sherwood Forest and the district of Bassetlaw north of Nottingham when he attended a jousting tournament at Blyth in June of the year 1256.

He stayed there for the next two months whilst being trained in the noble art of chivalry. His father also owned a house and park at nearby Hodsock, which Edward used to visit several time during his reign as King of England.

When Edward reached maturity and became King, he proved to be a strong and effective leader of the country. In his teenage years however, he upset a lot of people by his wild and irresponsible nature.

The historian Matthew Paris tells that most of Edward's friends were foreigners who encouraged him in many acts of lawlessness. Paris gave an example of the time they robbed and ill-treated the Monks at Wallingford Abbey.

Paris also told of an incident of brutality by Edward in which he met a young man by chance. He bullied and mutilated the man, just to amuse his friends.

Edward was related to Simon de Montfort because of Simon's marriage to his aunt, King Henry's sister. As a young man Edward was quite impressed by his uncle, and was on close and friendly terms with his cousins. In the year 1260 he knighted Simon de Montfort's two eldest sons Henry and Simon the younger.

Their parting of the ways came as the crisis over the Provisions of Oxford divided the two families, Edward and his cousins being forced into opposition against each other.

Simon de Montfort was born in France midway between Paris and Chartres and adopted England as his ancestral home. He did become more passionate in the cause of the English people than the native born English themselves.

There is still in existence a portrait of him in a window of Chartres Cathedral, in which he can be seen as a man in his early twenties, dressed in the armour of a knight. On reaching the age of twenty-one, Simon came to England to claim his inheritance, which in the absence of his family had been given by King Henry to the then Earl of Chester.

The Earl gave up his claim to Simon's lands, and on the 13th August 1231, King Henry confirmed that all the estates, which Simon's father had once held 'And which do belong to Simon by hereditary right', should be returned.

Simon served his King and country with honour both at home and overseas, and took part in a religious crusade to the holy land. On the 7th January 1238, Simon became a member of the royal family by marrying the King's sister Eleanor in a private ceremony at Westminster Abbey.

The following year Simon was to regain the Earldom of Leicester, Nottingham's neighbouring county, and stood as the godfather of King Henry's eldest son, Edward I

EDWARD I.

His home was at Kenilworth in the Midlands of England. It was a well-fortified castle surrounded by a lake, and was in later years to be the scene of one of England's most heroic and longest sieges when the castle was defended by Roger Godberd and his fellow outlaws.

King Henry found that even though Simon de Montfort was his brother in law he was not going to be a puppet of the King. Simon would often oppose the King for what he considered just and in the best interests of the country.

As the years passed the King came to have a fear and dread of Simon. Matthew Paris tells of an incident when the King became caught in a thunderstorm in London on the river Thames, and he decided to take shelter in the Bishop of Durham's house, where the Aldephi now stands.

By chance Simon de Montfort was staying there, and he came out to greet the King who was visibly shaken by the storm. Simon comforted the King and told him not to be afraid as the storm was now over.

The King surprised Simon by saying 'I do greatly fear thunder and lightning, but by God's head I fear thee more than all the thunder and lightning in the world.'

To which Simon replied 'Fear your enemies my Lord King, those who flatter you to your ruin, and not me your constant companion and faithful friend'?

The life of Roger Godberd does not appear to have been particularly affected in the early stages of the political manoeuvring between the King and his Barons.

In Nottingham however the tension was being felt. The town was to become involved in a struggle for power over the appointment of Sheriff's.

This saw the emergence into public life of two of the main characters in the Robin Hood legend, the knight Richard Foliot who was to help the outlaws in later life, and Reginald de Grey who became the Sheriff of Nottingham.

Under the Provisions of Oxford agreement the Baronial party was to advise the King on the appointment of officials. In the October of 1261, however the King issued a writ to the people of Nottingham and Derby ordering them to only obey his nominee of Sheriff, instead of what the King called 'The usurpers of the Office of Sheriff.'

The Barons firmly believed that Sheriff's should only serve for one year, and have to be elected by the freemen of each county. The King however, believed that only he had the right to appoint officials, and that they should serve him for as long as he so desired.

One of the last of the Baronial Sheriff's to serve in Nottingham was Sir Richard Foliot, our knight of the geste ballad. He was of course, the man who helped the outlaws when they were forced to live outside of the law.

Foliot was of a similar age to Roger Godberd, and once held land in Normandy, France. He gave up the land to King Henry, in return for an annual grant equal to the sum of seven pounds and payable for the remainder of his life.

Although Richard Foliot had residences in South Yorkshire and Derbyshire, his main home was a castle in Wellow on the northern edge of Sherwood Forest. He lived there with his wife and their son Jordan.

. He served the Barons well as their choice of Sheriff but an incident, which occurred in the year 1262, caused him to renew his loyalty to the crown. He became involved in a dispute with the people of Mansfield over a sum of money he had collected and kept. They said the money was for their use, and complained to the King.

He immediately handed over the money and swore an oath of allegiance to the King, promising in future to be the King's faithful servant.

As events were to show however, Foliot never lost his sympathy towards the Baronial cause.

Richard Foliot however, continued to have the respect of both sides in the conflict, and in the January of the year 1264, accompanied King Henry to Amiens in France. Foliot was there as a neutral observer of an arbitration award to be given by King Louis of France. The French King had offered to mediate in the bitter dispute between the English King and his Barons.

Also present at this gathering in Amiens was John de Grey, the father of Reginald our famous Sheriff of the Robin Hood legend. John de Grey came as a guarantor of King Henry's acceptance of the arbitration award.

John was one of the King's favourites, and first came to Nottingham in 1263, as the King's choice of Sheriff. John was born around the year 1200 and had a long history of service for his King and country, mainly as a Judge.

Under the Provisions of Oxford, he was chosen as one of the King's twelve representatives on the committee of 24 to administer the country. He also acted as a counsellor to the King's son. Edward.

It is not too surprising therefore, in view of Reginald's upbringing, that he should follow his father into public life. In the year 1264 he succeeded his father as the Sheriff of Nottingham, being in his mid twenties, one of the youngest ever Sheriff's to hold this prestigious office.

Henry Hastings was also at Amiens in France eager to hear the result of the arbitration award. The Barons were quietly confident that the French King would rule in their favour. When Simon de Montfort wasn't able to join them however, they should have sensed that fate was going to conspire against them.

On his way to France, Simon decided to visit Catesby Abbey near Northampton but unfortunately the horse he was riding fell. In the accident Simon broke his leg leaving him with no choice but to return home to Kenilworth and wait for news of the arbitration award.

Simon must have been devastated when he heard the news that King Louis had ruled in King Henry's favour, and overturned the Provisions of Oxford agreement.

What was to make the award unacceptable was not only the restoration of the King's power of absolute rule, but his right to use foreigners to rule England.

A happy King Henry returned to England with an army of French knights knowing that his Barons would find it difficult to accept the arbitration award. Henry did offer to meet his Barons at Oxford, but the meeting ended without any sign of a compromise between the two sides.

The English people however, were not prepared to go back to being treated as second-class citizens in their own country. Their feeling of frustration about the re-introduction of foreigners into England, led to a riot at Oxford University.

The prospect of a civil war seemed to be growing by the day. A prominent feature of this period of unrest was the way in which Robert Ferrers was able to continually get the better of Prince Edward.

Prince Edward's intense hatred of Robert Ferrers soon became evident during the struggle for power between the King and his Barons.

It was to be the King's continuing vindictive treatment of Robert Ferrers and of his followers, even after a peace settlement had been reached, that was to prolong Roger Godberd's outlaw life.

Edward marched his men to the city of Gloucester to punish the people there because Gilbert Clare, the Earl of Gloucester, had refused to swear an oath of allegiance to his father, the King.

Robert Ferrers, who was at nearby Worcester when he heard the news of Edward's attack, rushed to Gloucester to help the townspeople. On Ferrers arrival, Prince Edward quickly surrendered and accepted the Barons terms.

As soon as Ferrers men had withdrawn however, Edward took out his revenge on the townspeople.

On hearing the news of Edward's treachery, a furious Ferrers retaliated by marching his men to Prince Edward's stronghold at Chester.

A large royalist army may have defended Chester, but Robert Ferrers and his men soon took control of the city.

Edward responded by attacking Northampton castle held by Simon de Montfort's son, Simon the younger. He was helped by his uncle, Richard of Cornwall and after a short battle; young Simon surrendered, and was taken to Windsor castle as a prisoner. Following this victory the King made his way to Nottingham castle where he stayed as a special guest of John de Grey and our Sheriff, Reginald.

Prince Edward meanwhile, in the absence of Robert Ferrers, destroyed Ferrers castle at Tutbury and laid waste to the lands and crops of his tenants.

Edward then made his way to London hoping to gain the support of the Londoners, but he was too late because the Londoners had given their support to Henry Hastings. It was Henry Hastings who was to become a leading figure in the early development of the Robin Hood legend.

Prince Edward was also to see the unpopularity of the crown when his mother the Queen, was given a hostile reception as she passed through London.

In all this tit for tat, something had to give, and a civil war seemed inevitable. To avoid any confrontation with the King, Simon de Montfort decided it was in the best interests of the country to send the Bishops of Worcester and London, to discuss the terms of a peace settlement.

The Barons pledged their loyalty to the King, and said they had no desire to overthrow the throne, but to defeat his real enemies, his foreign advisors. The King was in no mood to compromise, leaving no option but for war.

Although Simon knew his men were outnumbered, there was no other way but to fight for their cause. After spending a night in prayer he called his men together the following morning and told them that they were not only fighting for justice, but for the future of democracy in England.

To boost their morale, and to emphasise the sacred nature of their cause, Simon told them to wear the white cross of the crusaders over their armour.

On that morning, the 14th May 1264 Simon marched his men into Lewes, a town near Brighton, on the south coast of England. Simon was unable to fight alongside his men due to his broken leg, so Henry Hastings and Gilbert Clare, the Earl of Gloucester, led the Barons into battle.

They gained an immediate advantage over the royal army by positioning their troops on the high ground. Their tactics worked to perfection and the royal army was easily defeated. After the battle Henry Hastings was rewarded for his bravery and distinction, by being knighted.

On the royal side, Prince Edward let his father down by recklessly chasing a group of fleeing Londoners for four hours. When he returned to the battlefield that afternoon, the fight was over and his father the King, a prisoner.

Edward surrendered and was held as a hostage on his father's good conduct.

On the following day Commissioners were elected to only appoint Englishmen as counsellors with the power to direct the King in all matters and to see that he no longer lived extravagantly.

Those of the King's supporters, who did manage to escape, made their way to France. It was feared for a while that they were gathering French support for an invasion of England. De Montfort decided therefore to keep both King Henry and his son Prince Edward under house arrest, and to strengthen his control of the shire counties.

To achieve this aim, Simon De Montfort sent instructions to John de Grey at Nottingham castle to hand over control of the castle to his son, Simon the younger.

It was from this particular appointment that both Roger Godberd and his brother Geoffrey came to be employed at Nottingham castle.

Simon de Montfort recruited men loyal to his cause. In Nottingham, John de Grey was to be provided with an armed escort not only for his safety in travel, but to ensure that he did not enter into any liaison with people hoping to overturn the gains of the Baronial party.

Following Henry's defeat at Lewes, the King ceased to reign except in name only. For the next 15 months Simon de Montfort became the virtual ruler of England.

The King accompanied Simon wherever he went, his role nothing more than to be available to put his seal on documents concerning the matters of state.

Prince Edward too was kept under check. He stayed for a while at De Montfort's home at Kenilworth castle. Edward was allowed to have visitors and to roam freely, but he was always kept under close supervision. This was to ensure that he kept his promise to abide by the agreement made at Lewes.

The people of England also saw democracy at work as Simon pushed ahead with his reforms. One of his first acts was to summon the 'Great Parliament' in which for the first time the cities and boroughs were able to send their own representatives.

During this brief period of peace and stability, our three main characters of the legend, carried on with their lives without any indication of what the future had in store.

Roger Godberd worked at Nottingham with the Sheriff, Reginald de Grey, whilst Richard Foliot completed the work on his castle home at Wellow and Grimston Park.

On his return home from the arbitration at Amiens in France Richard Foliot did not seem too concerned by the problems which had developed in England. He was more concerned with the task of improving his estate and manor at Wellow.

In the March of the year 1264, he applied for and got the necessary planning permission to enclose his castle home with a double ditch, and a wall of stone and lime. He was also allowed to crenellate his home that is to fortify it with battlements.

During the time of Roger Godberd's fifteen months of service at Nottingham, he does appear to have got on well with the Sheriff, Reginald de Grey. They had a shared love of hunting, and used to go hunting together in Bestwood Park in Sherwood Forest.

This enabled Roger to get to know Sherwood Forest well, which was to be a great asset to him in later years when he became a major outlaw.

Whilst they were hunting together, and on such friendly terms, Roger and the Sheriff were not against a bending of the forest laws whenever the occasion arose, or of even poaching the King's deer.

There is in fact, a public record in the Sherwood Forest records for the year of 1264, which tells of them being presented at court together for the offence of 'Theft of the King's Deer.'

The court record tells that Roger and the Sheriff stayed overnight at the garrison camp at Bulwell, a few miles to the north of Nottingham, and then went hunting in Sherwood Forest the following morning.

Their parting of the ways came in the summer of the following year 1265, when the Baronial movement began to crumble with a change of allegiance developing back to the King led by Gilbert de Clare. He had previously supported Simon de Montfort at the battle of Lewes.

Gilbert and Roger Mortimer, a well-known enemy of Simon de Montfort, joined together to help Prince Edward escape from his captivity. Their devious plan for Edward's escape was to send him a horse as a gift. Edward was then able to fool his guards by pretending to try out the horse, and then make a dash for freedom.

When Simon heard of the uprising against him, he told his son, Simon the younger, to gather together an army of volunteers. A large number of these were drawn from the East Midlands region, one of their most famous recruits being of course, Roger Godberd.

Our three main characters were divided by the political choice facing the country. Our Sheriff of Nottingham was a loyal servant of the crown, hardly surprising considering his family were in receipt of prestigious and important positions of state from their friendship with King Henry and Edward.

The knight Sir Richard Foliot decided to take a neutral stance and not commit himself to either side, but wait and see how the crisis developed.

For Roger Godberd the choice was straightforward. As he originated from the county of Leicester he believed that he owed some kind of loyalty to Simon de Montfort, who was after all his Lord as the Earl of Leicester. He believed that Simon was a man who had served the people well, and introduced good things in his reform of local government.

On the 31st July, Roger arrived in company with many other volunteers at Kenilworth castle, under the command of De Montfort's son, Simon the younger.

The recruits may have been tired and weary after their long march to Kenilworth, but their spirits were high.

They spend the evening feasting and drinking together in anticipation of what they believed would be a glorious victory over the royal forces, and the restoration of Simon de Montfort's full power and authority.

Prince Edward however had other ideas and put into action a very clever and devious plan.

He used scouts to follow Simon de Montfort as he travelled in the west, and to watch the gathering of De Montfort's reinforcements at Kenilworth.

Edward's plan was to isolate Simon and his men on the western side of the river Severn, thereby denying them access over the river, and to spring a surprise attack on the volunteer army at Kenilworth.

To achieve his first aim, Edward set about destroying all the bridges near the crossing at Worcester, and burning all the boats that Simon would have needed to ferry his men across the river.

Edward then sent an army to travel overnight and reach Kenilworth by the following morning.

Kenilworth may well have been a well fortified castle protected by a large surrounding lake, but the royal army was able to cause utter confusion and chaos.

Following on from the heavy drinking and celebrating the previous evening, Simon the younger and some of his men had foolishly decided to stay overnight in the priory rather then the safety of the castle walls.

Prince Edward's plan of delaying Simon de Montfort's reinforcements worked very well. Apart from being able to cause mayhem he was also able to take prisoner some of their leaders.

Roger Godberd was able to avoid capture, but Simon the younger only escaped by fleeing naked from his bed, and being helped to the safety of the castle.

Simon de Montfort meanwhile, found a way across the river Severn and decided to stay overnight in the Abbey at Evesham.

The Bishop made him welcome, but no one was aware of the impending danger to Simon's life.

By the morning of the 4th August Prince Edward had managed to surround the town of Evesham. He blocked the escape routes using Roger Mortimer's men on the bridge and his own and those of Gilbert de Clare on the top of the hill facing down towards the Abbey.

Edward then showed his deviousness by using the banners captured at Kenilworth to deceive de Montfort. His troops carried these banners towards Simon de Montfort's forces, making Simon believe they were the reinforcements from Kenilworth.

Simon's small force now completely outmanoeuvred and encircled by the royal troops. There was no Robert Ferrers to help, or the reinforcements from Kenilworth.

Some of Simon's men tried to cross the bridge but were cut down by Roger Mortimer's men. Simon knew that there was no way of escape, and that they would have to fight to the death. Henry Hastings tried to charge the royal lines and create a path through their ranks, but failed.

The following battle was fierce and short, with Simon being killed alongside his son Henry. His third son Guy and Henry Hastings, were captured and taken prisoner.

King Henry, who was at Evesham as a prisoner of Simon de Montfort, moved quickly to consolidate his control of the country.

Instead of offering a peaceful solution and uniting the country, King Henry decreed that all the lands and property of Simon de Montfort's supporters would be taken into the crown's hands. They were now known as the disinherited.

Roger Godberd and those followers who had survived the battle of Evesham had no choice but to continue their resistance. Although Roger had only fought in self-defence at Kenilworth, he was now forced to live as an outlaw.

The legend of Robin Hood was about to begin.

Chapter Three

Early life as an Outlaw

When Roger Godberd first heard about the death of Simon de Montfort and the events at Evesham, he was on his way with the other members of the army to meet up with Simon.

He was unaware of what had happened at Evesham until he met some of the fugitives of he battle coming the other way.

The men at Kenilworth had received a message from Simon saying he would be at Evesham, and they arranged to meet him there.

On that fateful morning of the 4 th August they set out for Evesham not realising the urgency of the situation or the danger that Simon was in.

After they had stopped at Alcester for refreshment, and were continuing their journey to Evesham, they met some of the survivors of the battle. They heard the depressing news of Simon's death, and the defeat of his troops by the royal army.

They told of the indiscriminate killing of Simon's men as they tried to flee the battlefield. Some people drowned trying to cross the river, whilst other men were chased and killed as they tried to hide in the fields.

Even those who sought sanctuary in the Abbey church and chapels, were pursued and killed where they stood.

Roger's feeling of sadness, at the deaths of Simon and his son Henry was made even worse when he heard that Simon's body had been shamefully dismembered even as he lay dead on the battlefield.

Prince Edward is said to have wept at the sight of his Cousin Henry de Montfort's dead body, but did attend the burial of Simon and Henry in the Abbey church.

So what were Roger and the other rebels to do? They decided it would be in their best interests to return to the safety of Kenilworth castle, and review their position.

At Kenilworth the young Simon was inconsolable with grief, and wouldn't eat for days. He felt he had badly let his father down in his hour of need.

As a leader and senior member of the rebels, Roger would have needed his diplomatic skills to avoid a backlash taking place. Some of the men wanted revenge for Simon de Montfort's death by executing the King's brother Richard of Cornwall.

He was being held in custody at Kenilworth castle as part of the deal to guarantee the King's observance to the Provisions of Oxford agreement.

After the events at Evesham, there were some people who wanted to kill him on the spot. Fortunately for justice, the wiser heads prevailed.

Richard was King Henry's brother and the second son of King John. He was named Richard in memory of Richard the Lionheart, and was known as the King of the Romans.

In the early stages of the Barons conflict, Richard took the side of Simon de Montfort against his brother, the King.

At the battle of Lewes family loyalty brought him back into the family fold. He fought alongside his brother in the losing battle, but after his surrender, became a prisoner of the Baronial party.

Following their victory at Evesham, King Henry and his son Edward didn't seem unduly concerned about Richard's fate.

King Henry decided to stay behind at Worcester whilst Edward by-passed Kenilworth, and went on to Nottingham castle. Prince Edward took with him many of the prisoners from Evesham, and on arriving at Nottingham, received a joyous welcome from John de Grey.

HENRY III. AND PRINCE EDWARD ENTERING THE TOWN AFTER THE BATTLE OF EVESHAM.

The public records do not reveal if our Sheriff Reginald de Grey helped Prince Edward in the raid at Kenilworth, and the battle at Evesham

It must be assumed that he did. He would not have sat idly by when the men from Nottingham castle deserted their posts to enrol as volunteers at Kenilworth.

It is also interesting that Edward headed straight for Nottingham castle after Evesham. Was Reginald with him?

Over the years Reginald proved himself to be a great military leader for his King and country. He was there for Edward when he helped him to conquer Wales, and in the many battles between England and Scotland.

The following year Reginald was to be rewarded by the crown by being given Nottingham castle. Nottingham was a royal castle with especially built royal apartments for when ever the King decided to stay there. Reginald was given the castle 'to keep at his pleasure.'

At Kenilworth, despite the defeat, there was a feeling of optimism that a general amnesty might be given to them by the King. They regarded themselves as patriots who were not opposed to the King, but his false foreign advisors.

Accordingly, both as a gesture of goodwill and to settle the impasse, they released Richard of Cornwall. It was on the understanding that Richard would help Simon's widow, and get them a sympathetic hearing.

It didn't take long for Roger and the other men to have their hopes dashed. The King insisted that the lands and tenements of every supporter of Simon de Montfort would be taken into the King's hands, thereby forcing the rebels to continue being known as the disinherited.

At Nottingham castle John de Grey had set up a court to try the prisoners. Those with property had it confiscated and those without any lands were sent to prison.

Simon de Montfort's widow was at Dover castle when she heard the news of his death, but when she was told that King Henry had created his son Edmund as the Earl of Leicester, and given him the lands of her late husband, Eleanor left the country forever.

Roger and the other outlaws left Kenilworth and set off to the north of Nottinghamshire, and the Isle of Axholme in the fens of Lincolnshire. It became the rallying centre for the outlaws because of its position as a safe haven.

Although it was not really an island being many miles inland, it was surrounded by water and marshes making it easy to defend against any would be attackers. The area soon attracted a large gathering of outlaws some having been helped to escape from their captors.

The only problem for the disinherited was the close proximity to the Isle of Henry of Almain. He was the Lord of the nearby manor of Gringley on the Hill, to the north of Nottingham in the district of Bassetlaw.

He was a close friend of Prince Edward, and one of those men who encouraged Edward to break his promise to the Provisions of Oxford.

Born in the year 1235, the eldest son of Richard of Cornwall, he had previously sworn an oath of allegiance to Simon de Montfort promising to never bear arms against Simon or his men. Simon told him, in what proved to be a good assessment of Almain's character, that he feared his fickleness and unreliability rather than his arms.

Henry of Almain fought at Lewes against Simon and the Baronial party, and had joined Prince Edward in the wild chase of the Londoners.

He was not present at Evesham, but had been given the manors of Tickhill and Gringley on the Hill, which had been taken from William of Furnival, one of Simon de Montfort's supporters.

In the middle of December and after having been warned of Prince Edward's impending attack on Kenilworth, Simon the Younger decided to leave Kenilworth.

There was still widespread support for the De Montfort cause throughout the country. There was Adam Gurdon, who was leading the rebels in the south of England, and John d'Eyvill and John Vescy in the north. Simon decided to join d'Eyvill and the outlaws on the Isle of Axholme.

John d'Eyvill was the Keeper of the northern Forests and held York and its castle on behalf of the de Montfort party. Although he was not at Lewes or Evesham he fully support the disinherited, and after de Montfort's victory at Lewes he was given the custody of Scarborough castle, previously held by Henry Hastings.

He also held some land in Nottingham at Egmanton, and his connection to the area can be seen with a stain glass window in the nearby church at Laxton displaying his coat of arms.

When Prince Edward heard of the whereabouts of the rebels he headed north and made an offer of peace, to Simon the younger in particular.

The outlaws were offered terms to settle if they would place themselves 'At the King's award and ordinance, saving life and limb and prison.'

Henry Almain offered to stand as a guarantor for the safety of young Simon, but the main question for Roger and the other outlaws was if his word could be trusted.

Young Simon did agree to go to Northampton castle, because Richard of Cornwall said he would speak on his behalf. Richard did appeal for moderation in the treatment of the disinherited, but was ignored.

The terms for the young Simon was to leave England forever, and a promise that in future he would do nothing to the detriment of the King.

As there was nothing on offer for the outlaws they decided that it would be safer for Simon to go to France.

Roger and his fellow m en would meanwhile, continue their life as outlaws until the day when a satisfactory and honourable peace deal could be achieved, and the young Simon allowed to return home to England.

John d'Eyvill was summoned to attend a court hearing at Windsor castle, but he refused to attend and continued his resistance in the northern area.

Shortly afterwards Simon was joined in France by his brother Guy. He was helped to escape from prison, which meant that there was now no member of the de Montfort family in England to lead the disinherited.

There was however good news for Roger and his men. Robert Ferrers, the Earl of Derby and Henry Hastings, had both been freed from their captivity. Roger and his men were only too eager to join up with Robert Ferrers at Duffield in the county of Derbyshire.

The young Ferrers led his men to great success, as he swept through the Derbyshire countryside taking all before him including the castle home of Sir John de Verdun, now a royalist supporter who once sided with Simon de Montfort.

There were numerous complaints to the authorities that Ferrers and his army were driving all the available livestock in the area into a special compound in order to provide food for his followers.

The importance of food supplies for a large army was not lost on Roger in the following year when he was the leader of the outlaws, and returned to Duffield where he knew his men would find food and supplies.

The disinherited continued their resistance with great success, and the various leaders, Robert Ferrers, John d'Eyvill and Henry Hastings decided it would be better to join together at Chesterfield.

The town of Chesterfield was situated twelve miles to the west of Sherwood Forest and the town of Mansfield.

On the 15th May, the year 1266, an army led by Henry of Almain, a constant thorn in the side of the outlaws, made a surprise attack on the headquarters of the outlaws.

Roger Godberd, his fellow outlaws, Henry Hastings and John d'Eyvill managed to avoid capture, with some people being safe because they were out hunting for food.

Almain meanwhile was able to capture Robert Ferrers because he had been forced to stay behind suffering from gout. Ferrers tried to avoid capture by hiding in the nearby church but Almain was able to find him and make an arrest.

Ferrers was bound head to foot in chains and taken to Windsor castle, never again to play any part in Roger's life.

The battle and capture of Robert Ferrers who was a very popular hero, has been commemorated by the church of St. Mary's in Chesterfield, known as the church with a crooked spire. The scene of the battle is depicted on a stain glassed window

As their cover had been exposed once again, Roger and his fellow outlaws were forced to move on, but this time there was a feeling of great euphoria and expectancy. The gossip and rumours spreading throughout the country, told of Simon the Younger planning to return to England.

Roger and Henry Hastings decided to lead their men to de Montfort's former home at Kenilworth castle, and wait for the young Simon's return. John d'Eyvill went back north.

We were now to see one of the longest and bravest sieges ever known in England, as the outlaws withstood the mighty onslaught of the crown forces for nearly six months.

Amongst the outlaws defending the castle, we had the camp followers including wives, girl friends and relatives of the men. One notable volunteer, who came and offered his support, was Roger's younger brother, William.

Kenilworth castle was a magnificent and well defended castle which was situated in the Midlands area of England. It had once been a royal castle and was given to Simon de Montfort as a suitable residence for the Earl and his wife, the King's Sister Eleanor.

The outlaws wisely prepared themselves for a long siege, by stocking up with a plentiful supply of both food and weapons. They didn't have to wait too long before King Henry arrived at Kenilworth castle with the royal army and his son Edmund.

King Henry had, as mentioned previously, created his son Edmund as the Earl of Leicester, in place of Simon de Montfort. He also gave Edmund the lands of the late Simon including the castle at Kenilworth.

Edmund however, was going to find it very difficult to claim his new inheritance as the outlaws frustrated all the crown's attempts to take the castle.

Although the outlaws were helped by the fact that a large lake surrounded the castle, they had to rely on the organisational skills of both Roger and Henry Hastings to overcome the many and varied methods of attack used against them.

The castle was constantly attacked on all sides but the attackers were always driven back. When their opponents erected wooden belfries to try and scale the outer walls, the outlaws always smashed them down.

When the royal troops used rowing boats to cross the lake they were always beaten back or had their boats sunk.

Edmund also brought up stone throwing machines to bombard the castle, but the outlaws had machines of their own and fired back at their attackers.

An eyewitness account of the siege describes some of the stone balls colliding in mid air, as each side hurled them at each other.

When Prince Edward arrived at Kenilworth to help his brother Edmund, he is said to have expressed admiration for the outlaws determination, and extraordinary courage in defending the castle against all odds.

The siege lasted for several months, but behind the scenes, attempts were being made to call a cease-fire.

The Catholic Church and the Pope in particular, took the lead in trying to arrange a peace settlement. The Cardinal Ottobuono came to England to negotiate a lasting peace, but it proved to be a difficult and frustrating task because of the hard line taken by King Henry.

The King eventually agreed to moderate his treatment of the disinherited. A committee of twelve was chosen to draft a plan suitable to both sides, but to be subject to the approval of the King and Henry Almain.

On the 31st October 1266, a treaty to be known as the 'Dictum of Kenilworth' was drawn up offering a ceasefire for the outlaws. They were given 40 days to reach a decision and the right to seek help from Simon the Younger.

It did seem at first as if the defenders of Kenilworth castle were going to receive an honourable settlement. On the 14th November Roger together with his brother William and Henry Hastings, applied to the court for their pardons.

They were allowed to leave Kenilworth without the fear of being arrested as the court allowed them the right of safe conduct in travel until the hearing of their case.

On the 12th December, the court granted Roger and William their pardons, but there was a price to pay for their freedom. The Dictum decreed that they would have to pay a fine based on the value of their land. The value of land was calculated as ten times its annual revenue. This figure was used as the basis of the Dictum with the fines being set at varying rates ranging from twice the annual revenue up to five times depending on each individual case.

Henry Hastings and Robert Ferrers were made exceptions to the general rule of the Dictum however, with their fine being set at seven times the annual value. The tenants of Robert Ferrers were also penalised vindictively by being denied any chance of a return to their former land.

Henry Hastings considered his terms unacceptable and he decided to continue his resistance by joining as their leader, those people still standing out on the Isle of Ely. This was a base in Cambridgeshire where the approaches to the city were surrounded by fens and water.

During their siege at Kenilworth the rebels had been heartened to learn that Ely had been taken by John d'Eyvill.

There was general feeling that the disinherited had not been given the honourable settlement they were promised and although Roger had been given his pardon, and could return to his life as a farmer, he had the dilemma of being left in charge of a large number of men. They had rallied around him in search of a decision of how to face the future and he felt duty bound to remain as their leader.

At this time, Roger was also involved in a dispute with the Abbott of Garendon Abbey. It finally ended in court action being taken against him by the Abbott.

The cause of the trouble was the land, which Roger had leased to the Abbey, and the money he had borrowed from the Abbott.

The Abbey of St. Mary's at Garendon also housed a convent where the nuns tended to the sick. It was situated to the east of Roger's home and some twenty miles south of Nottingham.

There is no indication whether the money Roger had borrowed was to help him whilst he was the run, or to pay his fine under the Dictum. It is clear however, that Roger wished to rid himself of his debt to the Abbey and take back the land he had leased to them

It may also have been that Roger needed the land to find employment and a home for his dispossessed followers, but whatever the reason, the Abbott refused to return the leased land. He had need of the land too, so that the lay brothers could continue growing food for the Abbey.

Roger took the law into his own hands and forced the Abbott to hand over the Deeds, which provided proof of the ownership of the land. He had second thoughts about the incident, because two days later he returned to the Abbey this time forcing the Abbott to sign a Charter of Quittance saying that the money which Roger owed had been paid.

The Abbott reported the matter to the authorities and a ruling was made in which Roger had to lease the land to the Abbey with permission for them 'to cultivate and use at their pleasure for as many years as they wished.'

Whilst Roger and his men remained as outlaws and the King was enriching himself at the expense of Simon de Montfort's supporters, the outlaws did have sympathisers in the country. Gilbert Clare, the Earl of Gloucester, may have turned against Simon de Montfort and helped the crown to defeat him at Evesham, but he did not approve of the way the crown were treating the disinherited.

Gilbert was in constant touch with Henry Hastings and John d'Eyvill at Ely, and was determined not to allow the King to defeat or further humiliate the rebels.

Roger meanwhile moved his men to Duffield, a castle home of the Earl of Derby, Robert Ferrers, situated some fifteen miles west of Nottingham hoping that Ferrers might gain his release from prison, and help his tenants to regain their former positions in the community.

Another factor for the move to Duffield was that Roger knew that there would be access to a plentiful supply of livestock, which he would of course need to feed his large number of men.

On their arrival at Duffield, Roger and his men were to find that the castle had been destroyed and burnt to the ground in an act of vandalism by the crown troops.

When Roger saw what had happened at Duffield, his emotions were a mixture of anger and frustration. He felt anger at the crown's treatment of Robert Ferrers, and that his former tenants had been exempt from the Dictum and therefore, unable to return to their former life.

He reasoned that if his men were going to be treated as outcasts and outside the law, they might as well lead a life as outlaws.

Accordingly, Roger led his men into a life of crime. They waylaid and robbed travelling merchants, members of the clergy, and those people who they considered to have been disloyal to Robert Ferrers.

It is not too surprising that the legend of Robin Hood began as the outlaws caused utter mayhem in and around Sherwood Forest and Nottingham in particular.

King Henry wrote to Roger Leyburn the commander of the royal army based at Nottingham expressing his concern at the number of robberies taking place in Nottingham, and that they were so serious as to threaten the town itself.

The outlaws so dominated the forest areas that when news of their activities reached Nottingham, there was a genuine fear the outlaws might overrun the castle.

As a precautionary measure, and for the defence of the castle, the authorities supplied timber for the building of wooden barricades as a defence against any attack, but as the outlaws continued to take the law into their own hands, the Nottingham authorities were forced into taking further action against them.

In the April of the year 1267 Roger Leyburn the justice of Sherwood Forest, set out in command of a large force to put an end to the outlaws activities.

13th Century Nottingham Castle

Roger Godberd and his fellow outlaws however, had shown during the siege at Kenilworth their fighting qualities against the best forces in the country, so the Nottingham men were not going to find it easy to deal with them.

The determination of Roger and the outlaws to avoid arrest soon became clear to Leyburn's men when the two sides met.

In the ensuing battle the men from Nottingham were easily beaten, and then made to pay for their audacity in disturbing the outlaws. Their horses were taken from them, and they had to make their own way back to Nottingham on foot.

At the same time as Roger's men were humiliating the troops from Nottingham Gilbert Clare the Earl of Gloucester was keeping the promise he made to help the rebels cause. Gilbert marched his men to London, and took control of the city. He was joined by John d'Eyvill who left Ely.

Gilbert held London until such time as King Henry III was prepared to compromise and to offer more favourable terms to the disinherited. Gilbert had involved himself in the dispute because he was annoyed at the crown's treatment of the rebels, and the broken promises he had been given

The Earl had fought alongside Simon de Montfort at Lewes, but had turned against him at the time of the battle of Evesham in return for a promise by Prince Edward to accept the terms of the Provisions of Oxford.

He now expected the crown to honour their promises, particularly the removal of all foreigners from office, and the return of the disinherited lands.

The King's brother Richard of Cornwall played a part in reconciling the two sides. Richard had always opposed the act of disinheritance, and urged his brother to relax his punishment of the rebels, and unite the country rather then continue with his policy of strife and disunity.

The clergy were also active in bringing about a peace, and set about raising money to help the disinherited pay their fines.

A sticking point for the disinherited was that under the Dictum of Kenilworth the fine levied upon them had to be paid before they could claim the return of their land.

Prince Edward was able to come to terms with John d'Eyvill and his friends who were given two assurances, immediate possession of their lands, and financial aid from the clergy towards the cost of their fines.

It was generally accepted however there could never be a lasting peace until such time as Henry Hastings ended his occupation of the Isle of Ely.

Prince Edward travelled north and reached a settlement with John Vescy. He was now free to turn his attention to the Isle of Ely.

Accordingly, he set off for Ely to bring an end to the continuing resistance of Henry Hastings.

Although the Isle of Ely was a difficult place to reach in those far off days, because the approaches to the city were surrounded by fens and water, Prince Edward was familiar with the area.

When Edward was 15 years old, he had accompanied his father King Henry to Ely to consecrate an extension to the Abbey.

Ely was famous for its cathedral and castle, which two centuries earlier had been the site of the Saxon Hereward the Wake's defiance of the Norman invaders led by William the Conqueror.

William the Conqueror had laid siege to Ely but could not subdue Hereward and his men. The standoff was only over after a negotiated settlement. The occupation of Ely by Henry Hastings was to end after the conclusion of a similar settlement.

Prince Edward and Henry Hastings reached an agreement. In order to settle the dispute which had plagued England for so long, Hastings swore on a bible, and set his seal to a document that he would never again bear arms against the King.

In return Henry Hastings was given back his lands and property and money from the church to pay his fine under the Dictum. Shortly afterwards in the November of 1267 he attended a Parliament held at Marlborough.

At this historic meeting, King Henry passed a statute making law almost all of the reforms originally demanded by Simon de Montfort. The main exception was that the King kept his right to choose his own ministers, and to appoint Sheriffs.

It meant that Simon de Montfort had not died in vain, and his fight for parliamentary reform had finally been won.

But what about Roger Godberd and his fellow outlaws? The civil war in England may have been over but Robert Ferrers, his tenants and supporters were still exempt from the Dictum. There was no help from the church for Robert Ferrers to have his fine paid, and being unable to pay he was eventually to lose his lands and property,

There were also no plans to reach an agreement with Roger and his men, and the authorities were in fact making plans for another attack on Roger and his fellow outlaws.

In the month of September 1267, a large army of men set out from Nottingham led by a captain, several knights, and up to 50 archers. The troops encountered the outlaws some twenty miles south of Nottingham, near to the home of Roger Godberd in Charnwood Forest.

Once again the outlaws proved their superiority, and after a brief and fierce exchange the Sheriff's men were forced to flee for their life back to Nottingham again without their valuable horses.

During this period, the life of our knight Richard Foliot was not particularly affected by what was happening all around him. He did find however that this year of 1267 was to be a difficult year for him. He completed the building of his castle home, but was then to become involved in a family crisis.

A few years earlier in the December of 1263, Richard had intervened to help one of his land workers, Thomas of Grimston whose son William was involved in a fight with a Richard of Stapleton who died of his injuries.

Richard Foliot pleaded on behalf of young William and got the young man a pardon on grounds of self-defence. Richard was now faced with a similar situation.

A man called Jordan had fought with and killed a man called John Bramwich. Foliot obtained a similar pardon for Jordan on the grounds of self-defence.

The original copy of the recording of this event, written in Latin, is intriguing. Was the 'Jordan son of" mentioned by the court scribe Richard Foliot's son Jordan?

Roger needed a new base as the clash in Charnwood Forest was too close to home for comfort.

In the October, November of 1267 the outlaws moved to Sherwood Forest and the manor of Mansfield where they were able to stay for the next four years. Henry Hastings had connections to the area, and it was here that they were able to find support and protection.

Sadly Henry Hastings was to die the following year in what seemed to be mysterious circumstances, but the help which the knight Richard Foliot was to give to Roger was to be the basis of a close friendship between the two men.

The outlaws completely dominated the Sherwood Forest region, and as the tales of the outlaws daring and total disregard of the law spread throughout the land, Roger's real name became forgotten as he acquired the nickname of Robin Hood.

How he came to be known by this particular name we will probably never know. During the 13th century Roberto was the popular name for any outlaw or thief being derived from the French word rober for a robber.

In the Geste ballad the chief characteristic of Robin Hood was the wearing of a hood, which he only removed when he was sure that the person being robbed did not recognise or know him.

When King Henry VIII used to dress up as Robin Hood he was always known to wear a hood.

Roger Godberd was of course well known in Nottingham because of the time he worked there under our Reginald de Grey, the Sheriff of Nottingham. The keeping of his identity a secret was therefore, of great importance.

Was he known as Roberto of the Hood and then quite simply, Robin Hood?

Another possibility for the origin of Roger's nickname comes from the historian Andrew Wyntoun who placed our outlaw as being alive in the year 1283, and the English poet Robert or William Langland.

Wyntoun covered the period of history up to the year 1406, and Langland who was born around the year 1330 is best remembered for his poem 'Vision of Piers Ploughman' in which he told of the rhymes of Robin Hood being well known throughout the country.

What is of particular interest however about Andrew Wyntoun's dating of Robin Hood being alive in the year of 1283, and a section of Langland's poem, is that it offers an insight into the term used by the authorities of that period to describe what could be our famous outlaws.

In his poem Langland refers to an outstanding outlaw and character by the name of Robberd the Robber, and his fellow outlaws as Roberdsmen, or Robert's men.

In the reign of King Edward III there is a reference in the Statutes of the year 1332, to the Statute of Winchester made in the year 1285.

It was stated that the Statute of Winchester had been passed in the year of 1285 in order to combat the felonies and robberies made in times past by outlaws known as Roberdsmen

Could it be that this description of the 'robber Godberd's men' was shortened to Roberdsmen? There were certainly no other major outlaws during this period of time.

How he acquired this nickname doesn't really matter as we now move to that time of his life in Sherwood Forest.

As he has become so well known as Robin Hood, we shall identify him by this nickname as the storytellers and wandering Minstrels did, rather than his real name of Roger Godberd.

Chapter Four

Life in Sherwood Forest

For an insight into Robin Hood's outlaw life in Sherwood Forest, we are fortunate to have the geste ballad.

Although the composer of the ballad is unknown, it is possible from the information provided by the storyteller to identify the period of time it covers.

The lives of the three main characters of the ballad when linked to the public records, begins in the October November the year 1267. It also describes in detail the final showdown between the outlaws and the Sheriff of Nottingham in the winter of the years 1271-1272.

It ends with Robin Hood's death twenty-two years after the end of his days as an outlaw in the year of 1293.

The ballad opens with an introduction by the storyteller as he calls his audience together to sing the praises of our famous outlaw.

'Come listen to me ye gentlemen'
'That be of freeborn blood'
'I shall tell you of a good yeoman'
'His name was Robin Hood'

'Robin stood in Bernesdale'
'And leaned against a tree'
'And by him stood Little John'
'A good yeoman was he'

The description of the outlaw's location as Bernesdale tells us that the ballad composer is describing the modern day district of Bassetlaw. It was originally identified in the public records as Bernesdelau.

As mentioned previously, the district was to the north of Nottingham, and included the northern part of Sherwood Forest in its boundary.

Roger needed a permanent base for his men. This he found at Perlethorpe, a short distance from the castle home of Richard Foliot and nearby Edwinstowe. It became known as Robin Hood's meadow. The outlaws could farm the land, graze their livestock, and grow hay to feed their horses.

The storyteller goes on to introduce some of the other outlaws.

'Also there was Will Scarlock'
'And Much the Miller's son'
'There was not much of his body'
'But he was worth a whole man'

In a conversation between Little John and Robin, John tells his master that it was time he had something to eat. Robin said that he wasn't particularly interested in eating until his men had apprehended a suitable victim for robbery.

The ballad then describes Robin's religious feelings and how he loved to take mass. This confirms John Fordun and Walter Bower's description of the time when Robin's determination to take mass, almost had him caught by the Sheriff of Nottingham.

This was because Robin would not leave the church until the service was over.

'Master, then said Little John'
'Before we eat out meal'
'Tell us where we shall go'
'And what life we shall lead'

Although the outlaws had found a new and settled home, their future life still remained uncertain.

The manner, in which John asked his leader how they were going to live and survive as they were living outside the law of the land, does show that this kind of life had not been planned, but forced upon them.

Robin however had every confidence that it was only a matter of time before they could return to their normal life. He explained what kind of standards he expected his men to live by, whilst they were living as outlaws.

'Do not worry said Robin'
'We shall do well enough'
'But do no harm to a husbandman'
'That tilleth with his plough'

'Nor do harm to a good yeoman'
'That doth walk in the greenwood'
'Nor harm a knight or squire'
'That would be a good fellow'

'But those Bishops and Archbishops'
'They you shall beat and bind'
'But the High Sheriff of Nottingham'
'Keep him well in mind'

Although Robin was a devout man he did consider that the robbery of certain members of the clergy was permissible particularly those who lived on the fat of the land, and took money from the poor.

He also gave a warning to his men to be wary of the Sheriff of Nottingham, indicating they were in an area under the control of the Sheriff of Nottingham. Robin was of course very familiar with the Sheriff, Reginald de Grey, from their days working together at Nottingham castle. He knew what a formidable opponent Reginald would be.

The ballad tells us that the outlaws had an unusual method of robbery, in which they only robbed those who had more than enough for their needs.

Robin would send his men out to apprehend a passing traveller, and bring them back to him as a guest. The victim would then be dined and fed well by the outlaws, before being made to pay well for their refreshment.

John was told to take Much and Will Scarlock with him and find a suitable candidate for robbery.

'Now walk up to the Saylis'
'And on to Watling Street'
'And wait there for some stranger guest'
'By chance you might them meet'

Saylis is the reference to the willow tree, and Watling Street was the name used in those days to describe the main road between Warsop and Worksop. This was in the Bassetlaw district of Nottinghamshire.

Perlethorpe is linked to Warsop, and the then Watling street by the river Meden, where willow trees can still be seen today growing alongside the river bank.

John and his fellow outlaws met a sorry looking knight who turned out to be Sir Richard Foliot.

'All dreary was his appearance'
'And little was his pride'
'With one foot in his horse's stirrup'
'And his other foot dangling beside'

'His hood hung over both eyes'
'He rode in simple array'
'A sorrier sight than he was'
'Rode never on a summers day'

Richard Foliot accepted an invitation to go with the outlaws and meet Robin Hood. This encounter was to be the start of a long and lasting friendship between our knight and the outlaws.

Richard told the outlaws that he had intended to dine at either Blyth or Doncaster. This information enables us to pin point the locality of the outlaws, because we are told on which road the outlaws were now on.

In the 13th century a new road had been built which ran from Nottingham to the north of the county. It passed straight through Sherwood Forest on its way to the north. It was known then as the road from Nottingham to Blyth and Doncaster, the road being better known today as the A614.

That part of the new road that ran through Sherwood Forest in the Bassetlaw district was parallel to, and a few miles from, the Watling Street that the outlaws were told to use as they set out to look for travellers to rob.

The outlaws must have started their journey on what is now known as the A60 and linked up with the nearby A614 road going towards Blyth.

In those days Blyth was a popular stopping place with travellers for food and accommodation.

Richard joined the outlaws for a meal.

> 'They washed and wiped themselves'
> 'And down to dinner sat'
> 'Bread and wine they had enough'
> 'And venison from a deer'
>
> 'Swans and Pheasants they had a plenty'
> 'And fowls of the river'
> 'And they never wanted for any bird'
> 'That was ever bred on a tree'

After the meal was over, Robin asked the knight to pay for the food he had consumed. He was however, a poor choice as a victim of robbery, because he had no money.

'But pay before you go said Robin'
'Me think it is only right'
'For it never was the custom'
'For a yeoman to pay for a knight'

'I have no money said the knight'
'That I may offer for shame'
'Go and look Little John said Robin'
'And never mind the blame'

'Tell me the truth to the knight said Robin'
'So God have part of thee'
'I have but half a pound said the knight'
'So God have part of me'

'If thou have no more said Robin'
'I will not take one penny'
'And if you have need of more'
'I freely shall give to thee'

The knight Richard was searched by Little John and found to be telling the truth about his poor financial position.

'Tell me one word said Robin'
'And in confidence it shall be'
'Were you made a knight of force'?
'Or else of yeomanry'

Knights of force were a feature of Henry III and Edward I's reign, confirming the ballad was set in the 13th century.

There were differing ways of becoming a knight. It could be obtained as a result of a person's inheritance or be granted by the King as a reward for services to the crown.

Land too played an important part in the way knights were created. In medieval England the way in which people held their land was based on the Feudal System, the name coming from the word Feu meaning a right to hold land in return for services.

The King held all the land but granted most of it to his Barons who in turn leased some of this land to other nobles or knights. In return for the use of the land the knight had to serve his Lord for 40 days a year. He had to be prepared for battle armed and on horseback and provide a specified number of soldiers.

There were the knights of force who came about their position because they held an estate worth twenty pounds a year, and the knights from yeomanry.

These were yeomen who tended to farm their own land and when the value of their land increased, they could be called upon to provide a knight's service.

This happened in later life to Roger Godberd's son when he inherited his father's land and was asked to serve as a knight.

Robin continued to question Richard.

'Or have you not managed well'
'And lived a lawless life'
'Or else in usury and debauchery'
'With wrong has lived thy life'

'By none of these things said the knight'
'Have I lived a life of sin'?
'For one hundred years or more'
'My ancestor's knights have been'

Richard explained to Robin that he was poor because of the help he was giving to his son.

'And in what manner said Robin'
'Have all thy riches gone'
'By my great folly and kindness great'
'I have lost them all he said'

'In truth Robin I had a son'
'That should have been my heir'
'And when but twenty years old'
'In a jousting field full fair'

'He slew a knight of Lancaster'
'And also a squire bold'
'And to save him in his right'
'My goods were set and sold'

'My lands were put in pledge Robin'
'Unto a certain day'
'To a rich Abbot here about'
'Of Saint Mary's Abbey'

In 1267 Richard Foliot had intervened to help a man named Jordan charged with killing a man called John Bramwich. Did the storyteller think this was Foliot's son Jordan?

Apart from the money Richard had spent to prove this man's innocence on the grounds of self-defence, Richard would also have been under financial pressure from the building work on his castle home.

In those days a source of borrowing money came from the wealthy Abbeys, who were often prepared to lend money to the local landholders. We also know that Roger Godberd had borrowed money from his local Abbey.

Robin showed the charitable side of his nature by lending money to the knight so that he could repay his debt to the Abbey. He would then have avoided the risk of having to forfeit his land and property.

'Go forth Little John said Robin'
'And go to my treasury'
'And bring me four hundred pounds'
'The money that is necessary'

'Is this wise, said Little Much'?
'John said what grieveth thee'
'It is alms to help a gentle knight'
'That has fallen in poverty'

'Master then said Little John'
'His clothing is so thin'
'You must give the knight a livery'
'To wrap his body therein'

'For you have scarlet and green master'
'And many a rich array'
'There is no merchant in merry England'
'So rich I dare well say'

'Give him three yards of every colour'
'And look that well measured it be'
'Little John took no other measure'
'Than his bow from a tree'

'And of every handful he measured'
'He leaped over feet three'
'What devil kin's draper said Little Much'?
'Thinkest thou to be'

'Will Scarlock stood still and laughed'
'And said with a knowing grin'
'John may the better measure give'
'For it did not cost him dear'

Little John could of course, afford to be generous with his measurements. This cloth would no doubt have been part of the many stolen goods that the outlaws had accumulated before moving to Sherwood Forest.

The first part of the ballad ends with Robin giving the knight a horse to carry all the goods he had been given, and the services of Little John.

'When shall be the day said the knight'
'Of my repayment be'
'This day twelve months time said Robin'
'Under this greenwood tree'

'I shall lend thee Little John said Robin'
'And he shall thy servant be'
'In a yeoman's stead he may well stand'
'If need for such there be'

The second part of the ballad only concerns the knight and the Abbott of the Abbey of Saint Mary. The time had arrived for the money the knight had borrowed from the Abbott to be repaid.

The Abbott however was hoping that the knight would be unable to repay his debt and have to forfeit his land.

'The Abbott said to his convent'
'As he stood on the ground'
'This day a year ago there came a knight'
'Who borrowed four hundred pound'

'He borrowed four hundred pound'
'Upon all his land so free'
'And unless he comes this very day'
'Dis-inherited he shall be'

When the knight eventually arrives at the Abbey with the money, he rather strangely pretends that he is unable to repay his loan and asks for more time to pay. The Abbott however does not have a charitable nature and refuses the knight's request for more time.

'The company were all at dinner sat'
'In the Abbott's hall'
'The knight came in and kneeled down'
'And then spoke to them all'

'Greetings Sir Abbott said the knight'
'I have come to hold my day'
'The first word that the Abbott said'
'Was have you brought my pay'

The knight asks for more time to pay but the Abbott is not very sympathetic to his problems. The knight then appeals to the chief justice who is there, but he is unable to help. The knight then placed four hundred pounds on the table and left the hall smiling. His debt repaid.

'Merrily singing he went home'
'As men have told the tale'
'And his lady met him at the gate'
'At his home in Verysdale'

Richard told his wife that he had settled accounts with the Abbott, and that they should give thanks to Robin Hood.

In the original hand written copy of the ballad it is difficult to correctly interpret the name the composer used to describe the knight's home. This is because of the closeness of the writing.

We know from the public records that Richard Foliot's castle home was in Wellow near to a Ferresdale, and that the medieval name of the valley in which both Wellow and Rufford Abbey stood, was known as Nettlydale.

In ancient documents relating to Rufford Abbey and Wellow, travellers were directed to the area by being told to look out for the signs to Nettlydale.

'The knight lived in quiet at home'
'The truth for to say'
'Until he had the four hundred pound'
'All ready for to pay'

The ballad moves on for twelve months to the time when the money owed by the knight has to be repaid. The knight set out to meet Robin Hood with the gift of one hundred bows and arrows.

He was delayed on his journey however, by stopping to watch a wrestling match. During this period wrestling was a popular form of entertainment.

'He came to a bridge where wrestling was'
'And tarried there a while'
'And there were all the best yeomen'
'Of all the countryside'

'There was a yeoman in that place'
'Who was wrestling in that strife'?
'But he came from far and had no friend'
'And nearly lost his life'

That particular yeoman who had caught Richard's attention was the outright winner of the competition. Because he was a stranger in the area, his opponents tried to deprive him of his prize.

The knight took pity on the winner, and intervened to see that justice was done. This worthy deed however, was to make him late for his appointment with Robin Hood.

In the third part of the ballad, the storyteller moves away from the knight and introduces a tale about the Sheriff of Nottingham.

The Sheriff watched Little John practising his archery skills, and he was so impressed that he invited him into his service. The storyteller also informs us that John was once an employee of the knight.

'Hearken and listen, Gentlemen'
'All that now be here'
'Of Little John who was the knight's man'
'Good mirth you shall hear'

'It was upon a merry day'
'That young men would shooting go'
'Little John said he would them meet'
'And anon he fetched his bow'

'Three times Little John shot about'
'And always cleft the wand'
'The proud Sheriff of Nottingham'
'By the marks did stand'

'The Sheriff swore an oath'
'By him that died on a tree'
'That this man was the best archer'
'That ever he did see'

The Sheriff asked Little John who he was, and where he came from.

'Tell me now young man'
'By what name are you called'?
'In what country were you born'?
'And where do you live now'

'I was born John said, in Holderness'
'If I may my mother believe'
'And when I amongst my kindred dwell'
'Men call me Reynold Greenleaf'

'Now tell me, Reynold Greenleaf'
'Will thou dwell with me'?
'And every year I will give thee'
'Twenty marks for thy fee'

'I have a master, said Little John'
'A courteous knight is he'
'And if he will grant leave of me'
'The better it may be'

'The Sheriff he got Little John'
'For twelve months of the knight'
'And he gave John a stout horse'
'To look well in his sight'

The reference to John being from Holderness is intriguing. In the year 1265 the Sherwood Forest records show there was a John of Holderness employed at Nottingham castle.

The storyteller then goes on to describe an incident involving Little John that occurred one day whilst the Sheriff was out hunting.

'It fell upon a Wednesday'
'When the Sheriff was a hunting gone'
'And Little John lay in his bed'
'And was forgot at home'

The real life Sheriff of Nottingham of our tale, Reginald de Grey was particularly interested in hunting. No matter what part of the country he was in, he always found time to sample the local hunting scene.

John overlaid, and when he awoke he was too late to be served any food. The butler refused to serve him until the Sheriff had returned home, and closed the kitchen door.

'John kicked the door with his foot'
'It opened up well and fine'
'There had been a large delivery made'
'Both of ale and wine'

'Little John ate, and Little John drank'
'As long as he pleased so to do'
'But the Sheriff had in his kitchen'
'A cook, stout and bold also'

The cook accused John of being rude and in the argument that followed a fight ensued. Although neither man was the winner, John was impressed by the cook's fighting qualities, and invited him to join Robin Hood and his fellow outlaws.

The cook agreed but before they set off they took with them as many valuables as they could carry.

'The silver vessels they took away'
'And all that they could get'
'Bowls, drinking cups and spoons'
'Not one did they forget'?

'Also all the money they took'
'Three hundred pound and three'
'And took them straight to Robin Hood'
'Under the greenwood tree'

There was in fact an outbreak of stealing and vandalism at Nottingham castle at the time when people abandoned their posts at Nottingham, and went to Kenilworth in support of Simon the younger.

When the crown gave Reginald de Grey Nottingham castle after the conflict was over, they agreed to pay for the damage done to the castle.

On Little John's arrival, Robin asked him if he had any news from Nottingham.

'What tidings come from Nottingham'?
'Little John tell thou to me'
'And greetings to the Sheriff'
'Who has sent you here to me?'

'His silver vessels and his cook'
'And three hundred pound and three'
'It was never by his good will'
'That these goods have come to me'

'Little John then there bethought'
'Of a shrewd and cunning plan'
'So off he set of his own goodwill'
'And five miles into the forest he ran'

'Hunting there with hound and horn'
'The proud Sheriff he did meet'
'And Little John in courtesy'
'Did kneel at his feet'

Little John tricked the Sheriff by telling him he had seen a large number of deer in the Forest.

'Yonder I saw a right fair hart'
'His colour was of green'
'And a fine herd of seven score deer'
'Are with him to be seen'

'Their antlers are so sharp master'
'I dare not shoot for dread'
'They are so large that I feared'
'I would be stricken dead'

The Sheriff's curiosity was so aroused that he willingly rode off with John running by his side, to find and see these deer for himself.
The Sheriff was unaware however, that John was leading him straight to Robin Hood, and that he would be forced into spending the night with outlaws.

'The Sheriff rode and Little John'
'On foot did run full smart'
'But when they came before Robin'
'John said here is the master hart'

'The Sheriff was to supper set'
'And served with silver white'
'But when his own vessels he saw'
'For sorrow he could not eat'

'Make good cheer said Robin Hood'
'Sheriff for charity'
'And for the love of Little John'
'Thy life is granted to thee'

After their meal was over and the day had come to an end, Robin ordered his men to take off their clothes and wrap themselves in blankets.

This was to show the Sheriff what a hard life it was, now that they had to live as outlaws in the forest.

'All night lay the Sheriff'
'In his breeches and his shirt'
'It was no wonder lying there'
'That his sides did hurt'

'Make the best of it, Sheriff'
'Said Robin for charity'
'This is the way we live our life'
'Under the greenwood tree'

'This life is harder said the Sheriff'
'That that of any hermit or friar'
'For all the gold in merry England'
'I would not long dwell here'

'For the next twelve months said Robin'
'Thou shalt dwell here with me'
'I shall teach thee proud Sheriff'
'An outlaw how to be'

The Sheriff was not very happy at the prospect of living this life and begged Robin to let him return home to Nottingham castle.

'If I have to spend another night here'
'Then Robin I beg thee'
'Cut off my head this very morn'
'And I will forgive thee'

'Let me go free said the Sheriff'
'For Saint Charity'
'And the best friend you ever had'
'I will be to thee'

Robin however, informed the Sheriff that he could only go free if he promised to never pursue the outlaws.

'Thou shall swear an oath said Robin'
'On my bright sword'
'That you will never waylay me for harm'
'Either by water or by land'

'And if you ever find any of my men'
'Either by night or day'
'Upon your oath you shall swear'
'To help them as you may'

The Sheriff was happy to agree. It is clear from the ballad that the outlaws' base camp must have been in Sherwood Forest as the Sheriff, who had been hunting in Sherwood, had only travelled a few miles to the camp.

The storyteller then moves on to the time the knight is expected to repay Robin the money he borrowed.

Little John was feeling hungry after the fresh woodland air had sharpened his appetite and told Robin that it was time to dine.

Robin said he was in no mood to eat because he was worried that the knight was not going to come.

'Worry not master said Little John'
'Sunset is not yet due'
'The day is not yet over, and I swear'
'The knight is trustworthy and true'

In the meantime Robin decided to send his men out to find any passing travellers, who would be likely candidates for robbery.

On reaching the highway the outlaws came across a large party of men passing through the forest, led by two monks dressed in black of the Benedictine order.

During their conversation with Little John they insulted Robin by calling him a thief and a man of ill repute.

This angered Little John who called the monk a liar, and during a skirmish that followed, one of the monks was killed. Their armed guard then ran off leaving the other monk and his two servants at the mercy of the outlaws.

'Much was ready with his bow'
'And the arrow sped away'
'It struck a monk upon his breast'
'And on the ground he lay'

'Of the fifty two strong young men'
'There stayed not a one'
'Save a little page and groom'
'To lead the pack horses with John'

John brought the monk to meet Robin.

'Robin put down his hood'
'When he the monk did see'
'But the monk was not so courteous'
'And let his own hood be'

'He is an ungracious man, Oh master'
'Then said Little John'
'It is no wonder said Robin'
'For courtesy he has none'

'How many men said Robin'?
'Had this monk with him, John'
'Fifty and two when we met'
'But many of them are now gone'

'Let us blow a horn said Robin'
'That our fellowship he may know'
'Then seven score of strong yeomen'
'Came running in a row'

'Each of them good clothes they had'
'Of scarlet bright and gay'
'They all came to good Robin'
'To hear what he would say'

The monk was invited to dine with the outlaws, and during their conversation he was told of the incident concerning the money, which the knight Richard owed to the Abbott of Saint Mary.

'They made the monk wash himself'
'And down to dinner sit'
'Then Robin and Little John'
'Served him with honour fit'

'Feed well monk said Robin'
'Thank you sir said he'
'And where is your Abbey said Robin'
'And who your patron Saint be'

'Saint Mary's Abbey said the monk'
'Though I be of humble rank there'
'In what office asked Robin'
'Sir, the high cellarer'

The high cellarer kept the stores of food and drink. As he was also responsible for the financial affairs of the Abbey, Robin asked if the monk knew anything about the money the knight Richard had borrowed.

'The Abbey has a surety said Robin'
'Between a knight and me'
'Of money that I lent him'
'Under the greenwood tree'

'The monk he swore a full great oath'
'With a sorry cheer'
'Of the money that you speak'
'I never before did hear'

Robin asked the monk how much money he was carrying, and that he would help him if he were in need. The monk however lied by pretending he only had twenty marks. In those days a mark was worth about two-thirds of a pound.

'What is in your coffers said Robin'
'Truly tell to me'
'Sir he said, just twenty marks'
'Is all I have with me'?

'If there be no more said Robin'
'I will not take one penny'
'And I'm willing to lend you more'
'If thou hast need of any'

'But if I find more said Robin'
'You might consider it gone'
'Apart from your basic need monk'
'You will have none'

Robin told Little John to search the monk and see if he was telling the truth about the money he was carrying. The outlaws were surprised to find that the monk had more than eight hundred pounds.

Robin therefore, decided to punish the monk by taking away all his money, just as he had promised if the monk was telling lies.

'The monk put spur to his horse'
'No longer would he abide'
'Drink a parting cup said Robin'
'Before you further ride'

'Not before god replied the monk'
'I regret that I came here'
'For much cheaper I may have dined'
'In either Blyth or Doncaster'

Robin jokingly replied.

'Greet well your Abbott said Robin'
'And your prior too, I thee pray'
'And bid he send me such a monk'
'So rich to dinner every day'

After the departure of the humbled monk the knight Richard arrived with the money to repay his loan to Robin. As mentioned previously Richard was late because of the help he had given to the wrestler.

'Now let us leave the monk awhile'
'And speak then of the knight'
'Who came to hold his day'?
'Whilst it was still light'

'He went straight on to Bernesdale'
'Under the greenwood tree'
'And there he found bold Robin Hood'
'And all his merry company'

'Have you your land again said Robin'?
'The truth tell thou to me'
'Yes before God said the knight'
'And for that I thank thee'

'Be not grieved I'm late said the knight'
'At a wrestling match I passed'
'I saw a young yeoman suffering wrong'
'And there did him assist'

'Now before God said Robin'
'For that deed I thank thee'
'The man that helps a good yeoman'
'His good friend then I'll be'

Richard gave the outlaws a gift of bows and arrows, and offered to pay the money he owed. Robin told him to keep the money after telling him of his encounter with the monk'

'When Robin had told his tale'
'They laughed and had good cheer'
'But by my troth said the knight'
'Your money is ready here'

'Keep it and use it well said Robin'
'Buy horses and harness good'
'And gild thy spurs all new'
'And if you are ever short of money'
'You can always come to me'

Roger Godberd may well have been a popular hero in Sherwood Forest as Robin Hood, but everyone in the region did not make him welcome. He was given a hostile and unfriendly reception as told in the ballad known as 'Guy of Gysebourne.'

The ballad may well be an exaggerated account of the incident that took place between Robin and Gysebourne, but the ballad must be respected because of its antiquity.

The Sherwood Forest records of this particular period certainly confirm the existence of a Robert Gysebourne whose last duty on behalf of the crown was in the year 1268. In the following year he received a pardon for the death of a Ralph Chatte. This was the time when Godberd and his fellow outlaws were most active in the region.

Robert Gysebourne did live near to the outlaws' base in the market town of Warsop situated in the northern part of Sherwood Forest.

It would of course have been almost impossible for anyone living in the Sherwood Forest district during their outlaw life, not to have been aware of their presence. The local gossipmongers would have made sure of that.

Roger and his fellow outlaws do appear to have been generally accepted by the local people, but to people like Robert Gysebourne and the members of the establishment he would have been an undesirable character.

The Gysebourne family carried out numerous duties on behalf of the crown mainly at King John's palace at Clipstone just a short distance from their Warsop home. The palace was used to carry out the legal requirements of the King in Sherwood Forest.

Warsop was near the castle home of Richard Foliot, and where the outlaws carried out their robberies. It is not too surprising therefore, that one-day Gysebourne and our famous outlaw would meet.

The storytellers have developed the ballad's interpretation of the confrontation between our outlaw and Gysebourne, in which Gysebourne was killed, into a tale of Robin being able to outwit the Sheriff of Nottingham.

Before the fateful encounter with Gysebourne, Robin had a premonition of his life being in danger, especially after a dream in which he was overpowered and beaten by two men.

When Robin told Little John of his dream, John told him not to worry as dreams very rarely came true. Shortly afterwards whilst walking in the forest with John, Robin's sense of foreboding returned, when he saw a man standing alongside his horse with a sword and dagger by his side.

John noticed Robin's apprehension at the sight of the stranger. Little John told his master to stay behind whilst he approached the man, and found out what he was doing in the forest.

Robin as an implication that he was a coward took this act of chivalry by John the wrong way. He angrily told John that he didn't need any man to protect him, and after a few harsh words had been spoken, Little John called Robin an ungrateful man, and then walked off in a temper, leaving his master behind.

Robin's curiosity about the man however, had now been aroused; particularly in view of the bow the man was carrying. Robin walked up to the stranger and asked if he was a good archer.

In the course of their conversation the stranger said he was looking for the notorious outlaw known as Robin Hood. He asked Robin if he could help him to find this outlaw.

Robin suggested that they had an archery contest first to decide whom, was the better archer. He told the stranger that later on he might be lucky and meet the outlaw he was looking for.

No matter how hard the stranger tried he couldn't match Robin's skill with the bow. When the contest was finally over, the man praised Robin by saying that he must be as good an archer as that notorious outlaw Robin Hood.

He thanked Robin for his hospitality, and said that he was determined to find and kill the outlaw Robin Hood.

The stranger asked Robin to tell his name, but Robin refused to do so until the stranger had first revealed his. He said that he lived in the forest, and then told Robin that his name was Gysebourne.

Robin told him that he too lived in the forest, and that he was the Robin Hood of Barnesdale that Gysebourne was looking for.

The facial expression of Gysebourne was to change into one of hatred, and when he drew his sword, a fight to the death began.

During the fight Robin stumbled and fell to the ground, but fortunately for him he managed to roll over and avoid Gysebourne's sword. Robin then jumped to his feet, and struck Gysebourne with a fateful blow.

Robin marked Gysebourne's face so that he would be unrecognisable. He then put his dead body on his horse, and set off to find his fellow outlaws. Robin said.

'For I will away to Barnesdale'
'To see how my men do fare'
'He set Gysebourne's horn to his mouth'
'And a loud blast it did blow'
'It was heard by the Sheriff of Nottingham'
'As he leaned under a tree'

This tale again shows that the Barnesdale of the ballads was in the north of Nottinghamshire, and in an area under the control of the Sheriff of Nottingham.

When earlier in the ballad John left in a temper, he set off for Barnesdale and whilst there was captured by the Sheriff of Nottingham.

When Robin arrived, he was surprised when he saw Little John being held in captivity by the Sheriff. He devised a plan to rescue John by changing his clothes with those of Gysebourne.

The disguise must have been very effective because even John did not recognise him. Robin told the Sheriff that the dead body he was carrying was that of Robin Hood and in return for the body, he asked for and got the release of Little John.

There are a number of ballads telling of Robin Hood's exploits, some probably true, and other exaggerated tales made to amuse an audience.

They majority revolve around the constant theme of Robin seeking out and testing men who had a reputation of being strong and bold.

Well-known examples are his meeting with Little John, when neither of them would give way and let the other pass over a bridge.

Then there was Friar Tuck, acknowledged as being a fierce and fearsome fighter. Robin made the Friar carry him over a stream, but the Friar retaliated by tipping Robin into the water. John and Friar Tuck were both invited to join the outlaws.

But all good things must eventually come to an end. The outlaws could not expect to disregard the law of the land forever. The Nottingham authorities however did admit that the only way they could defeat the outlaws, was to find men who were brave and fearless.

The person, who was chosen to lead such men in the final showdown against the outlaws, was Reginald de Grey.

Chapter Five

The Final Showdown

During the latter stages of Robin Hood's outlaw life, our Sheriff of Nottingham, Reginald de Grey, had left Sherwood to become the Chief Justice of Chester.

Chester was in those days an important port, and the gateway to the country of Wales.

In Reginald's absence from Nottingham and the Forest of Sherwood, the outlaws were a law unto themselves and they completely dominated the forest area.

The arrival of a relative of the knight Richard Foliot however, was to complicate Roger's life.

He was Walter Denyas, sometimes known as Euyas, who came to the area following the charge of killing a man.

Denyas received a pardon, and Richard Foliot agreed to stand bail for him and to guarantee his good conduct, but Denyas was a rule unto himself.

He was described in the public records as a man of violence and a robber and thief, who was eventually caught and executed in the year 1272.

During his time with Richard Foliot and the outlaws it does appear that Denyas was responsible for giving away the location of the base and hideout of the outlaws. This was in two separate incidents concerning the authorities.

In the first incident Denyas joined Roger Godberd and four of the outlaws as they left the castle home of Richard Foliot and travelled through the grounds of Rufford Abbey.

On reaching North Laithes Grange, a farm used by the monks of Rufford Abbey, the outlaws were set upon and captured by a royal army, and then taken as prisoners to Nottingham castle. How long they were held there, and how they got free we do not know.

It would of course be in keeping with the legend to believe that Little John and his fellow outlaws were able to help them escape with much sword fighting, abseiling down the castle walls and then dashing away on waiting horses.

There is in fact a ballad known as Robin and the Monk in which Robin was helped to escape from Nottingham castle by Little John.

It is however more realistic that Richard Foliot simply obtained their release by applying for bail on their behalf.

In another incident, which was to bring trouble to the outlaws, Denyas was chased through Sherwood Forest by an army led by a Roger le Strange. Denyas and his men must have been outnumbered by the troops because they were chased for many miles.

Denyas led his men to Perlethorpe, the outlaw's base camp, were he knew that Godberd and the main bulk of the outlaws would be, and thus able to help him.

And help him they did, because le Strange's troops were routed, and in the ensuing battle they had 16 of their horses taken from them.

Their total disregard of the law of the land eventually forced the authorities to take action as the complaints about their activities grew. It was said that no travelling merchants or members of the clergy were safe from robbery.

There was a major incident concerning a robbery at Stanley Abbey in Wiltshire in which a monk was killed, and Godberd was in later years to be charged with this robbery.

The authorities knew it would take a special body of men who were not only fearless, but willing to take up the challenge of bringing down the outlaws.

This recruitment would of course not come cheaply if you wanted the best. There was also the need of a great military leader, and what better man was there, than the former Sheriff of Nottingham, Reginald de Grey.

The East Midlands counties of Nottingham, Leicester and Derby joined together to share the cost of assembling this mighty force. Nottingham provided 40 per cent of the cost, and the other two counties 30 per cent each.

There had never been such an arrangement to help defeat such a large gathering of outlaws, but then again, Robin Hood and his followers were an exception to the rule.

Reginald de Grey was more than happy to take on the task of confronting the outlaws, and in the winter of the years 1271 and 1272, the final showdown between the outlaws and the former Sheriff of Nottingham was about to begin.

The geste ballad describes in detail this showdown. In the fifth part of the ballad, the tale begins with the Sheriff breaking his promise to the outlaws that he would not harm them.

He decided to hold an archery contest, with the prize for the winner being an arrow of both silver and gold. The Sheriff reasoned that Robin and his men would be unable to resist the challenge, thereby giving him an opportunity to capture them.

The former Sheriff of Nottingham certainly knew the outlaws well, because they did indeed find the challenge to be irresistible.

'A right good arrow the winner shall have'
'With the shaft of silver white'
'And the head and feathers of gold'
'Never in England would there be the like'

'When Robin heard the news'
'Under his favourite tree'
'He told his men to be ready'
'For that shooting to see'

'When they came to Nottingham'
'The targets were fair and long'
'And many were the archers bold'
'With bows looking good and strong'

'And when they had all shot in turn'
'Those arrows good and fine'
'Without doubt the first and best'
'Was indeed, our Robin Hood'

When Robin went to collect his prize however, the Sheriff's deception came into being. Attempts were made to capture the outlaws but after a fierce battle the outlaws managed to escape. In the skirmish Little John was injured in the leg and he told Robin not to compromise his escape, or that of the other outlaws.

'Robin saw the ambush broke'
'In the greenwood he would have gone'
'For many an arrow there was shot'
'Amongst that company'

'But Little John had been hurt sore'
'With an arrow in his knee'
'And he could neither go nor ride'
'It was a great pity'

Little John then begged Robin to kill him because he did not want the Sheriff to take him as a prisoner.

'I could not slay thee said Robin'
'That I could never do'
'For all the gold in merry England'
'If it were laid in a row'

'God forbid said Little Much'
'That died on a tree'
'That ever thou should, Little John'
'Part from our company'

'Much took John on his back'
'And carried him many a mile'
'Many a time he laid him down'
'And paused to rest a while'

There is no way of knowing if this incident concerning the archery contest actually happened, but the storyteller then goes on to describe events which can be confirmed by the public records.

The outlaws were pursued to the castle home of our knight Richard Foliot who gave them protection from arrest by the Sheriff'. Richard Foliot's castle is described in detail as being surrounded by a double ditch, and walled off from the road.

'Then they came to a castle strong'
'A little within the wood'
'Double ditched it was about'
'And walled off, by the road'

'And there dwelled the gentle knight'
'Sir Richard of the Lee'
'That Robin had lent his money too'
'Under the greenwood tree'

The castle home of Richard Foliot was in a district known in his lifetime as Thurgaton and Lye, alternatively as Lee. It was close to Sherwood Forest, and although Thurgaton still exists as a district, Lee has disappeared from the records.

'In he took good Robin'
'And all his company'
'Welcome be thou Robin Hood'
'Welcome thou are to me'

'I love no man in all this world'
'As much as I love thee'
'Worry not about the proud Sheriff'
'For safe here you will be'

'Shut the gates and draw the bridge'
'And let no man come into here'
'For the next few days you stay with me'
'To eat, drink, and have good cheer'

Reginald de Grey however had other ideas. He was not going to give up the capture of the outlaws easily, and the chase was on. Reginald was going to prove a very able and difficult opponent.

'Full fast his men came to the Sheriff'
'Men from the country called to arms'
'And they besieged the knight's castle'
'And the walls all around'

'The proud Sheriff, loud did shout'
'And said thou traitor knight'
'You keep here the King's enemy'
'Against the law of right'

'The knight said I would answer'
'That what I have done is right'
'And upon all the lands I have'
'That I am a true knight'

We know from the public records that Reginald de Grey was given instructions and money to recruit a force to take on the outlaws, and arrangements were made for the arrest of Richard Foliot for having given aid to the outlaws.

The description in the ballad of Robin Hood finding refuge and protection from arrest with the knight Sir Richard does correspond to what actually happened between our three main characters of the legend, Godberd, Foliot, and the Sheriff Reginald de Grey.

The public records also tell of Richard and Walter Denyas fleeing from Foliot's Wellow home to find shelter in his other home at Fenwick in Nottingham's neighbouring county of Yorkshire. Richard Foliot had previously lived in Fenwick which was some 50 miles north of Nottingham, before moving to Wellow.

Richard Foliot may have been out of the jurisdiction of Reginald de Grey but he was not to avoid the arm of the law as Reginald gave instruction to the Sheriff of York to arrest him.

Foliot gave up his son Edmund both as a hostage and a guarantee that he would attend a court to answer the charges of aiding the outlaws.

He did attend a court hearing charged with sheltering Denyas, Godberd and the other outlaws. Fortunately for him, the man leading the case was his old friend Gilbert de Clare, the Earl of Gloucester, who had previously helped the disinherited to obtain justice.

It is not surprising therefore that Foliot was acquitted of all charges. Meanwhile Reginald turned his attention to capturing Roger Godberd, and for the first time he had the outlaws on the run.

Reginald was to eventually arrest Roger and took him to the castle stronghold of Bridgnorth, some eighty miles west of Nottingham and forty miles south of Chester.

The castle at Bridgnorth was a formidable place being situated high up on a mount with a commanding view of the surrounding countryside. Anyone visiting or attempting a rescue would have been seen many miles away by the castle guards. It was a very safe place indeed, to hold an important prisoner.

We are not sure if rescue attempts were made by the other outlaws to release Roger but in the following year he was transferred to Chester, and then to the stronghold at Hereford on the border with Wales.

The storyteller goes on to tell of an incident involving the arrest of the knight by the Sheriff, and of a vicious clash with the outlaws in which the Sheriff was killed.

There is no record of a Sheriff being killed in office, so could the storytellers have confused an incident between a group of men led by Roger Godberd's brother Geoffrey and the servants of the de Grey family?

John de Grey, Reginald's father, and one time Sheriff of Nottingham had died from natural causes, and his widow sent her servants to Leicester on an errand.

They unfortunately met and clashed with Geoffrey Godberd and others who were carrying axes, knives, bows and arrows, and other weapons.

In the bloody fight that followed, a death did occur on the Sheriff's widow side. A Thomas Huchun was killed, and another man maimed.

Geoffrey Godberd then sought sanctuary in Leicester Abbey before being imprisoned.

Reginald de Grey was certainly alive and well during the final showdown with the outlaws, and destined in later years to serve his country well as a great military leader.

Roger Godberd's life as an outlaw was effectively over, and it was not until the year 1276 that he was finally able to gain his release.

This was because he had to wait for the return of King Edward to England, from the religious wars the crusades.

Edward became King on the death of his father Henry III in the year 1272, but he was unable to take the crown because of his absence from the country.

On Edward's return to England one of the outstanding problems was over the disinherited. The matter had never been completely settled and there were several outstanding matters to be resolved.

A special court was set up at the Tower of London to deal with these matters and this included Roger Godberd's offences.

The Sheriff of Hereford was given instructions to deliver Roger to Newgate prison in London, to await his trial at the Tower. Roger was charged as being a notorious bandit who was responsible for having committed several burglaries, murders, fires and robberies, in the counties of Nottingham, Leicester and Wiltshire.

The reference to Roger having committed offences in Wiltshire is very intriguing, because he was never known as having travelled so far south. It was the three East Midland counties of Nottingham, Derby and Leicester alone, who were asked to finance the army for the capture of Roger.

Roger was later charged with having led an attack on Stanley Abbey on horseback, and that during the ensuing battle a monk was killed. Roger denied the charge which leads one to suspect the possible involvement of Walter Denyas. He held land in the area and may well have been in dispute with the Abbey. Did Roger escort Denyas on this long journey south, but then things got out of hand?

We know that Denyas was caught and executed, but that Roger was never charged with this offence at Stanley Abbey until after the death of Denyas.

Did Denyas incriminate Roger with the authorities in order to try and save his own life?

King Edward reminded the justices at the Tower of London to distinguish between offences committed in times of war and offences committed in times of peace.

Roger Godberd's offences were committed under the guise of war and subject to the Dictum of Kenilworth and as such, did not involve loss of life or a long imprisonment.

Those persons including Roger Godberd who were in Axholme, Kenilworth and Chesterfield were to be dealt with in accordance with the peace made with them under the Dictum of Kenilworth.

The basis of Roger's defence was that he admitted the offences charged up to the time of the conflict with Simon de Montfort. Roger said that Edward's father, when he was King, had welcomed him into his peace, and pardoned him for whatever he had done against the peace.

He produced letters patent testifying to this fact and said that he will always be faithful towards the King and his heirs.

Roger reaffirmed that he was not guilty of the other charges, and that he would place himself upon the mercy of the King and country.

The courts gradually freed the disinherited, some on the payment of a fine, and they were allowed to return to their place in society. Their war was finally over.

Roger Godberd was never to be an outlaw again, and he retired to a quiet life on his family farm until his death in the year 1293.

Little did Roger know that he would become a national hero known throughout the world as Robin Hood, and that his life as an outlaw would never be forgotten in the minds of each new generation of people.

Chapter Six

Development & Distortion

We know that for over two hundred years following Robin Hood's death, all the historians and writers who wrote about his life were all agreed that he was a real person and an outlaw in the second half of the 13th century.

In the 16th century however, things began to change, as the legend became a victim of its own unique popularity.

During this particular period of time the popularity of Robin Hood was at its peak with May games and an annual festival being held in his honour. The festival was held on the first day of May each year, and the people took the day off to attend the festival and pay homage to Robin Hood.

This public celebrating of Robin Hood inevitably led to exaggerated tales and untruths being told about him. The storytellers of the day were happy to satisfy the interest in Robin Hood by telling new and fanciful tales of his life.

The result of this change saw the legend falling into two quite separate and distinct parts.

In the first part we have the life of Roger Godberd. He became known as Robin Hood and was responsible for the beginning of this most extraordinary legend as revealed by the early historians, public records and ballad composers.

In the second part particularly from the 16th century on, the legend gradually departed from its origins and roots. He was changed into a mythical figure by the writers of each succeeding century.

They tended to invent their own particular theories of his life and times, without any regard to the truth, or to any facts that could be proven.

The first change in the direction of the legend came in the year of 1521 from the Scottish historian John Major.

John Major had a book published called 'History of Great Britain' in which he placed the era of Robin Hood into that of King Richard the Lionheart.

Richard I, was the King of England during the years 1189-1199, and earned himself a reputation as one of his country's most popular hero's, even though he was absent from England for most of his reign.

Although Major disapproved of Robin Hood's lifestyle he did have a certain admiration for him. He described him as a most humane outlaw and the prince of all robbers who would never take money from the poor, or allow any woman to be ill-treated.

What is surprising is that John Major's description of Robin Hood was in accord with the geste ballad. This told us that at the end of Robin Hood's days as an outlaw it was a King Edward on the English throne not a Richard.

Major's failure to give any explanation for the change in the dating of the legend has prompted the 'Chronicle of Scottish Historians', and its review of his work, to sum up his theory as follows.

'As he doth guess'

There is also no mention of Robin Hood's name in any of the works of the national historian of the time, Roger Wendover. He covered the period from 1188 until his death in the year 1235.

He was located for many years at Belvoir priory near Nottingham, and would therefore have known our outlaw well, if of course he had existed during his lifetime.

Major's misleading theorising about Robin Hood was to have a far-reaching influence on the future development of the legend as his name now began to be associated with that of King Richard the Lionheart.

A wave of speculation was set off about the legend and in the years 1540 and 1569 we had two writers, John Leland and Richard Grafton accepting John Major's dating of the legend and adding a new dimension with a claim that Robin was a man of royal blood.

They did not however; state what title if any, he was supposed to have. They then confused the legend even more by giving completely opposite versions of his locality, and the reasons for him becoming an outlaw.

John Leland, who was an antiquarian during the reign of King Henry VIII, claimed that Robin Hood lived as an outlaw because of his dis-satisfaction with corrupt local law and administration.

He surprisingly placed the locality of the outlaws as not being in Sherwood Forest, but in a forest area some sixty miles north of Nottingham. This was in Nottingham's neighbouring county of Yorkshire. Leland also chose to completely ignore the cornerstone of the legend, the Sheriff of Nottingham, who had no authority in that area.

Leland provided no proof to support this new theory, and seemed quite content to hide behind the rather bland statement, 'What people say.' He did not say who these people were, or on what grounds they had based their judgement.

Leland, who was born around the year 1506, was a scholar in both Latin and Greek. On finishing his education in Paris, France, he acted as a tutor to the youngest son of the Duke of Norfolk. He became in favour with the court of King Henry VIII, after writing in flattering terms about the King.

In return for having given the King many books as gifts, Leland was rewarded by being appointed 'The Keeper of the King's library.' He later became the King's antiquary, a position that had never existed before.

In addition Leland received a payment to travel throughout the country in a search for English antiquities.

In the 16th century visit of Leland, Sherwood Forest would have been unrecognisable from the days of Robin Hood and the outlaws. Most of the old oak trees had now disappeared.

Sherwood had been heavily deforested over the years not only to provide timber for the building of the nation's sailing ships, but also to satisfy the ever-increasing demand for additional farming land.

During his tour of northern England Leland suggested that a wood and forest he found between Wakefield and Huddersfield was in his opinion, the main haunt of Robin Hood and his fellow outlaws.

He further claimed that our famous outlaw had met his death at nearby Kirklees Priory, a myth that was to continue for many years.

The interest of King Henry VIII was soon aroused after Leland had made his claims. The King made a special point of visiting the area with a Bishop Tunstall.

They described the area as 'one of the greatest and richest valleys in Europe' although it is not at all clear which region they actually visited, or what possible connection it had, if any, with the Robin Hood legend. It all seemed to be nothing more than a figment of John Leland's imagination.

He had a sad end to his life when he was declared mentally insane, and died in the year of 1552 without ever regaining his sanity.

A few years later the legend was taken into a different direction to that of John Leland.

Richard Grafton a prosperous London merchant and printer claimed that Robin Hood was a man of noble birth, who because of his wild living and excesses had lost his inheritance through debt.

Grafton was also to claim that on becoming outlawed Robin Hood sought refuge in Sherwood Forest and Needwood Forest, which was forty miles south of Nottingham in the county of Staffordshire.

Needwood Forest is by chance, where Robert Ferrers the one time leader of the outlaws, once held land and a castle at Tutbury.

Although Grafton always described himself as a grocer he is best remembered as a royal printer and publisher. In the year 1537 he acquired the right from King Henry VIII to print the new bible in English.

The King also ordered that every Parish in the country should buy a copy. In the year 1547 Grafton was granted the right, as the King's printer, to print the statutes and acts of Parliament.

Following the death of King Henry and his son Edward the accession to the throne of King Henry's daughter Mary brought about many changes in the administration of the country. Grafton became out of favour with the new Queen, and not only lost his position as the royal printer, but was imprisoned for a few weeks.

He is also well known for writing books on historical matters, but he did receive a lot of criticism in his lifetime by writers such as Stow and Buchanon. They accused him of slander and exaggeration in his writing.

In his book 'Chronicle at Large and mere History of the Affairs of England' Grafton gave the impression that his knowledge of Robin Hood's life was based on the public records. He claimed he had found Exchequer Rolls and old and ancient pamphlets which recorded the confiscation of Robin Hood's land and property,

He also claimed to have seen a document in which the King 'On being offended by Robin Hood's robberies' offered a large sum of money for his capture.

This was supposed to have taken place during the reign of King Richard the Lionheart.

These claims however, cannot be taken too seriously. The documents on which he based his dubious claims cannot be found, and there is also no record of anyone else saying that they too had seen the documents in question.

Richard I, who is always described as the Lionheart because of his bravery, succeeded his father Henry II as the King of England in the year 1189, but only spent a few months of his ten-year reign in England. He was either fighting in the crusade wars or living in France.

As we have mentioned earlier there was a connection to Nottingham and Sherwood Forest with King Richard and his brother John.

John had a hunting lodge in Sherwood Forest known as his palace, and King Richard did visit Nottingham castle and spend a day hunting in Sherwood Forest, which he said he enjoyed. This visit of course happened in the previous century to the real Robin Hood.

This constant fantasying and creation of myths about Robin Hood by the historians particularly in the 16th century prompted John Sheldon the Keeper of the Public records in the tower of London to make the following comment. He lived during the years 1584 to 1654.

'There is more historical truth in many of the
old ballads than in many modern histories'

What is so disappointing is that the myth about Richard the Lionheart being part of the Robin Hood legend still persists today. In the numerous films and television programmes made about of Robin Hood the constant theme is the placing of his lifetime into that of King Richard.

By the end of the 16th century the old style minstrel was becoming virtually extinct. Visits to the theatre, and the performance of plays, now became a more popular form of entertainment for a better-educated and more sophisticated population.

The tales of Robin Hood proved to be an ideal subject for the stage and in the year 1598 there was a performance on the London stage of two plays by Mundy and Chettle.

The theme of the plays consisted of the rehearsal of a play at the court of Henry VIII and by his special command. The title was 'The Downfall of Robert Earl of Huntingdon, Afterwards called Robin Hood of Merry Sherwood.'

The writers, not too surprisingly in view of the change in attitude towards the legend, set the play in the reign of King Richard the Lionheart.

In a romantic and tragic tale, the first scene tells of Robert's uncle, the prior Justice Warman, conspiring with the Sheriff of Nottingham to force our hero into a life as an outlaw because of the money he owed to his uncle.

Both Friar Tuck and Little John help Robert to escape from the clutches of the conspirators, and make his way to the safety of Sherwood Forest.

In a tragic ending both Robin Hood and Maid Marian died through being poisoned.

Although the play is nothing more than a fictional tale for the amusement of the audience, the use of the title Earl of Huntingdon for our outlaw is very significant.

This is the first time that anyone had given the name of a royal title for Robin Hood. In the 12th century reign of King Richard the Lionheart the title Earl of Huntingdon was a royal title used by the family of the King of Scotland.

The last Englishman to hold this title was the Saxon Waltheof who had been executed by William the Conqueror for his continued resistance to the Norman invaders.

Whether it is coincidence or not the title Earl of Huntingdon can be associated to Sherwood Forest and the Robin Hood legend. This is through Henry Hastings who was the leader of the disinherited.

In the year 1238 his father was appointed the Lord of the Manor of Mansfield in Sherwood Forest, and through his mother Ada, the young Henry did have pretensions to the title of the Earl of Huntingdon.

She was the daughter of David the Earl of Huntingdon the brother of the King of Scotland.

In the late 13th century Henry's son John made a claim to the title, which did in later years; revert back to an English title and to the Hastings's family.

In that part of the play where Robin was forced into becoming an outlaw, Little John was to tell his master,

'And I at Mansfield will await your coming.'

Michael Drayton, an antiquarian and poet from the period late 16th and early 17th century, composed a poem, which Drayton called 'Polyolbion', a Greek saying meaning rich in blessings.

In the 26th part of the poem he described the delights of Charnwood Forest, the home of Roger Godberd, before moving to Sherwood Forest, and singing the praises of Robin Hood and his men.

'To Sherwood still retired his only standing court'
'Whose praise this Forest doth pleasantly report'
'The merry pranks played would take an age to tell'
'And the adventures strange that Robin Hood befell'

'In Mansfield many a time for Robin hath been laid'
'And tricked all those who would have him betrayed'
'How often he hath come to Nottingham disguised'
'And cunningly escaped, being set to be surprised'

Michael Drayton was in no doubt that Robin Hood was a Nottingham based outlaw, in his poem 'Ballad of Agincourt.' This was about the famous battle between the English and the French in the year 1415, which the English won, thanks to the skills of their archers.

Drayton described the various flags and banners that were on display on the battlefield by the English counties. He made the following observation of Nottingham's banner.

'Old Nottingham, an archer clad in green'
'Under a tree with his drawn bow stood'
'Which on a chequered flag far off was seen'
'It was the picture of old Robin Hood'

The national popularity of Robin Hood, and the continuing interest in the legend led to his association with differing parts of the country he was supposed to have visited.

At Birchover, in Nottingham's neighbouring county of Derbyshire, there are some large stones amongst a group of rocks known to the local people as 'Robin Hood's Stride.' It is said that he once lived there.

Equally fanciful is that a bay came to be named after him on the northeastern coast of England between Whitby and Scarborough.

We were expected to believe that during a sea voyage he used his bow to good effect to kill the crew of a pirate ship and steal their treasure.

Nottingham too could see the tourist potential of Robin Hood all those hundred of years ago.

They claimed to have ancient relics of him including his bow and arrows. They however, considered that the most important item of all was his chair. The author Broome, told in his book 'Travels over England,' of a strange ritual that took place in Nottingham.

He said that having pleased ourselves with the antiquities of Nottingham we took horse and visited the well, and ancient chair of Robin Hood. This was not too far from hence, and the Forest of Sherwood. Being placed in the chair we had a cap they say was his, placed on our heads.

Having then performed the usual ceremony befitting so great a solemnity, we received the freedom of the chair and were incorporated into the society of that renowned brotherhood.

The writer Robert Dodsley also told us of a visit he made to Nottingham in his book 'Travels of Tom Thumb all over England and Wales.'

He told of his delight in visiting a site in Sherwood Forest, which he described as being not far away from the city of Nottingham.

Dodsley said that whilst he was in Sherwood Forest he was privileged to have seen a chair and a bow and arrow all of which once belonged to Robin Hood.

Apart from these items we also had another writer named Hutton, who referred in his book 'Journey from Birmingham to London' in the year 1786. He too claimed to have seen ancient relics of Robin Hood. He said,

'I was pleased with a slipper belonging to the famous Robin Hood, shown me fifty years ago at St. Anne's Well near to Nottingham, a place on the borders of Sherwood Forest to which Robin Hood once resorted.'

There was once an annual event, which used to be held by the Nottingham authorities at a site known as Robin Hood's Well. The Nottingham local dignitaries used to take part in a ceremony, which included much merrymaking.

The highlight of the day's proceedings was the honour of being allowed to sit in Robin Hood's chair.

A licence was always granted for the selling and drinking of wine and beer. Unfortunately one year the drinking got out of hand, and a near riot ensued with Robin Hood's chair being broken.

The shocked Nottingham authorities decided to cancel the ceremony forever because of the bad behaviour of all those present.

All the items which survived the melee, and were once supposed to belong to Robin Hood, were sadly sold off to a London theatre.

In the year 1795 the antiquarian Joseph Ritson tried to put some kind of order into the legend. He put together all the ancient and more modern ballads about Robin Hood and attempted to provide a detailed account of the outlaw's life and times.

Ritson did however warn his readers that he was not offering an authentic account of Robin Hood's life, but what information he had for their enjoyment.

He gave a quotation to summarise the many theories he had encountered.

'Some are good, some are middling, and some bad, but yet, they were the best that could be had.'

In his deliberations however, Ritson relied too much on the unproven theories of the 16th century writers, and failed to use the public records to authenticate or disprove the many theories he used.

Born in the October of the year 1752, in the north east of England at Stockton on Tees, Ritson spent most of his working life in the conveyance of land and property.

He settled in London and in the year 1780 set up in business at Grays Inn, where he qualified five years later as a lawyer.

Ritson had a fascination with English literature and history, particularly the ancient ballads. As a consequence he spent much of his life studying and writing on the subject

The great writer Sir Walter Scott told of his admiration for Ritson's dedication to the subject, but accused him of being too fastidious and pedantic in his attention to minute details. Ritson's critics also accused him of having,

'Printed indiscriminately, all the spurious trash which had accumulated over the years about Robin Hood's name.'

The build up of Ritson's mythical Robin Hood came to be the prototype of our outlaw's present day image. It began with the claim that Robin was born around the year 1160 in Lockesley in Nottinghamshire, and lived until the year 1247.

The source for this period of lifetime for Robin Hood came from the suspect Sloane manuscripts. The reference to his birth in Lockesley was contained in the disreputable and misleading 17th century ballad, 'Robin Hood's Birth, Breeding, Valour and Marriage.'

Not too surprising there is no trace or evidence of any such place as Lockesley in Nottinghamshire. It did however inspire Sir Walter Scott to create his fictional character the Earl of Lockesley in his tales of 'Ivanhoe.' These were loosely based on the exploits of Robin Hood and his men.

Ritson also took up the theory that our outlaw was a man of royal descent, who had pretensions to the title of the Earl of Huntingdon. He added that our outlaw's real name was 'Robert Fitzooth' which had been corrupted over the years into the name of Robin Hood.

The use of the name of Robert Fitzooth came from an 18th century theory by a William Stukeley. He attempted to prove that the Fitzooth family tree traced back to Waltheof, the last Saxon to hold the title of the Earl of Huntingdon.

On investigation the family tree was found to be false and a figment of Stukeley's imagination.

On examining the public records however, it is possible to find in the Magna Britannia, that there was a family by the name of Fitzooth in the 12th century. They lived in a Loxley in the county of Warwickshire. There is no evidence to suggest that they were ever involved in any outlaw activity. All that the pubic records do reveal is that they gave a portion of their land to the priory of Kenilworth.

Ritson also told of Robin Hood living to an old age and that on becoming ill, he met his death through the treachery of a female relative.

This event was supposed to have occurred in the year of 1247 at a Kirklees priory. Robin, on feeling ill, decided to visit the priory for the purpose of being let blood.

In medieval times, and even up to the 20th century, bloodletting was considered to be a cure for most ailments, and as a preventative form of treatment.

The visit of Robin Hood to a nunnery was taken out of context from the geste ballad, which said.

'By a woman, beguiled was Robin'
'A woman full of sin'
'The prioress of Kirkley'
'That nigh was of his kin'
'Then spoke good Robin'
'In that place where he stood'
'Tomorrow I must to Kirkley go'
'To be skilfully let blood'

Robin Hood's death was attributed to him having been bled to death by his relative the prioress. It was also claimed by Ritson, even though there is no mention of it in the geste ballad, that he was buried under some trees in the grounds of the priory where he died.

Another falsehood is that there was a stone epitaph placed on Robin Hood's grave, which was said to have the following inscription.

'Here underneath this little stone'
'Lies Robert Earl of Huntingdon'
'Never an archer were as he so good'
'And people called him Robin Hood'
24th Kal Decembris 1247

The stone epitaph and theory that Robin Hood's death took place at Kirklees priory near Wakefield, is yet another myth created about our outlaw.

The first writer to refer to Kirklees priory as being the site of Robin Hood's burial was of course, John Leland in the year 1540. As he made no reference to an epitaph, one can assume that it never existed in his lifetime

The mention of the name Earl of Huntingdon on the epitaph exposes it as a 17th century hoax. The year 1598 and the play by Mundy and Chettle, was the first time that this royal title had been associated with Robin Hood.

Further discrediting of the hoax appears in Gough's 'Sepulchral Monuments' in which he told of a stone, but that the epitaph was never on it.

The final proof of the creation of a myth came from the digging up of the ground by the owner of the premises, the late Sir Samuel Armitage. He had the ground dug up a yard deep to either prove or disprove the belief that Robin Hood was buried there. No bones were found, and it was noted that the ground had never been dug up previously.

The mid 19th century saw another change in the direction of the legend when a Joseph Hunter claimed that Robin Hood was a 14th century outlaw from Wakefield in Nottingham's neighbouring county of South Yorkshire.

As discussed in the opening chapter, this theory is a very strange one indeed. It would have meant Robin Hood being alive during the lifetime of the national historian John Fordun who made it quite clear that Robin Hood was born in the previous century to himself.

As we move to the twentieth century and more modern times, the popularity of Robin Hood has never ceased. With the advent of films and television the legend was the ideal medium for an adventure story.

Robin Hood was cast as a dashing and swashbuckling hero. The period was set in the 12th century reign of King Richard the Lionheart with the outlaws fighting injustice and the evil Prince John, and equally evil, Sheriff of Nottingham.

Unfortunately, the many films of the adventures of the outlaws' bear no comparison to the original tale.

The continuing fascination with the legend saw a claim that he could be a man by the name of Robert Hobbehod. He had been made a fugitive in York in the year 1225 over the non-payment of a sum of money.

The court scribes of the day had shortened his name in the public records to Hod that seemed sufficient reason for some people to claim he was the real Robin Hood.

There is however no connection in his life to being the leader of any gang of fellow outlaws, or of any involvement with Sherwood Forest and the Sheriff of Nottingham.

The continuous state of confusion in the legend had prompted some writers into a suggestion that Robin Hood is based on a partly fictitious character that has gradually evolved over the years. This is from the merging of various outlaws who acted outside the law of the land.

In Robin Hood however, we are not dealing with a fictitious character. Fictitious characters come from fictitious places, and in the case of Robin Hood he is associated with a real location of Sherwood Forest, and equally real person in the Sheriff of Nottingham.

Another character that some writers have suggested as a possible candidate for involvement in the legend is a Fulk Fitzwarin. He was outlawed during the reign of King John before receiving a pardoning in the year 1203.

He was a friend of King John as a young man but after an argument was stripped of his family holdings and took to the woods as an outlaw. Fitzwarin spent some time abroad and has no connection to any of the Robin Hood locations such as Nottingham or Sherwood Forest.

It is also claimed that the activities of the 14th century rebels the Folvilles, in association with the murderer James Cotterall could have had an influence on the Robin Hood legend. This too cannot be accepted as a possibility.

Apart from their being no similarity in their life as outlaws, the Folvilles operated against the law of the land during the 14th century lifetime of John Fordun. He was of course the earliest writer about Robin Hood who told us that the legend of Robin Hood was very well known, and established throughout the land, many years before the Folvilles had become outlaws.

The most fascinating feature about Robin Hood is that the interest in his life has captured the imagination of each new generation of people. It does seem that the immense popularity of Robin Hood has led to him becoming the man people want him to be rather than the man he really was.

The modern thinking in the legend is dominated by the belief that Robin Hood is somehow from Nottinghamshire's neighbouring county of Yorkshire where he is supposed to have been an outlaw in the 14th century. This is of course, far too late for the real outlaw.

The theory is based on the belief that the Barnesdale of the ballads is near Doncaster in south Yorkshire and not Nottinghamshire. Have they confused the real Robin Hood with the fictitious hero Ivanhoe who Sir Walter Scott placed in this area?

This area was identified in Robin Hood's days as the district of Strafforth, but there is no record of the name of Strafforth ever appearing in any reference to Robin Hood.

The belief that there was a Barnsdale Forest is also false. During the years of 1289 and 1290, King Edward 1 took time out to visit every Forest in England. The list of all the Forests in England does not mention a Barnsdale Forest.

There are also claims that a small village, now known as Barnsdale Bar could be the Barnsdale of the ballads, but this was never a forest area only an open area of moor land that acquired its name centuries after Robin Hood's death.

In the Geste ballad, a document that is used by many people to base their theories, does not mention the name of Barnsdale. On every occasion in the original copy of the Geste ballad, we are told that the location of the outlaws is Bernesdale not Barnsdale.

Did the ballad composer change the ancient name of the Bassetlaw district of Bernesdelau into Bernesdale to rhyme in verse?

When the ballad tells us that the outlaws are sent out to commit a robbery they are warned to avoid the Sheriff of Nottingham. Why should this warning be necessary if they were not in an area under the control of the Sheriff of Nottingham?

The Geste ballad also appears to place the outlaws in the Bassetlaw district of Nottinghamshire, when Little John is told to go and find a suitable candidate for robbery.

'And walk up to the saylis'
'And so to Watling Street'
'And wait there for some stranger guest'
'By chance you may him meet'

Saylis is the descriptive term for the willow tree, but some people claim that it is Sayles, an area of land in Yorkshire. This cannot be so because later in the ballad Robin tells John to walk up to, and under the Saylis. He wouldn't have been expecting his men to walk under a field, but rather under the overhanging branches of the willow trees.

The outlaws' base camp at Perlethorpe is linked to Warsop by the river Meden, where willow trees can still be seen today alongside the river bank. The road from Warsop to Worksop was also known as Watling Street.

A lone voice against what appeared to be a never-ending creation of myths about Robin Hood appeared in an article in the March issue of the 'Westminster Review' in the year 1844, when an anonymous writer expressed his anger at the continuous distortion of the legend.

He found it unbelievable that anyone could link Robin Hood to a royal title particularly as the ancient ballads had been consistent in their description of him as a yeoman, the skill with the bow being the trademark of a good yeoman.

The reviewer told of his sadness, that the man, who had resisted the destroyers of Simon de Montfort, and struggled so gloriously during the latter part of the 13th century in a fight for political reform and democracy, should have had the cause and period of his outlaw life forgotten.

The writer commented on how the memory of Simon de Montfort and his followers had faded in the minds of the people as each century passed by. He said how the many distortions of the tale had severed Robin Hood's link to the past, and had now lost its historic meaning.

He added that Robin Hood had become a mysterious figure and totally different character to what he really was, causing many people to believe that he was nothing more than a myth.

It is a little sad therefore, that the origin and roots of the legend have been forgotten, particularly when the real story is just as exciting as the fictitious one, if not even more so.

Chapter Seven

Conclusion

When Roger Godberd and his followers lived as outlaws, they could never have imagined, not even in their wildest dreams that they would become so popular and be forever remembered by each new generation of people.

Not only have they become national heroes, but also their fame has spread worldwide. The Sheriff of Nottingham too, has become as equally famous as the outlaws.

Although the tales of Robin Hood and the outlaws are so well known, no one has surprisingly given any details of what happened to them in their later life.

So what happened to our three main characters when the days of the outlaws were over?

Our knight Richard Foliot kept his position of favour and high standing with the crown authorities, in spite of his involvement with the outlaws. He spent the remainder of his life carrying out legal duties on the crown's behalf. This was in the Bassetlaw region, and at Lincoln castle.

As a reward for his services to the crown he was in the year 1277 given two live bucks and ten live does. This was to increase the stock of deer in his Park at Wellow.

Some years later in the year of 1290, Richard Foliot was given the custody of Horsley castle in Nottingham's neighbouring county of Derbyshire, and then a few months later, granted the right to hold a weekly Thursday market.

Although there was no register of deaths in this period we know that Richard died in the year 1299.

The law required the holding of a post mortem inquest to settle any tax liabilities that may be owed to the crown, and to confirm the legal transfer of the deceased person's property to their heir.

The property of Richard Foliot was transferred to his son Jordan, but his unfortunate son was to die three weeks later. The crown did however consent to his widow being given the right to remain at the castle home in Wellow.

Although the castle is no longer in existence, the land is known today as 'Jordan Castle Farm' and the distinctive feature of a double ditch can still be seen.

Our former Sheriff of Nottingham Reginald de Grey led a life of great service and honour for his King and country. He was a great military leader who helped King Edward I to take control of the country of Wales.

Reginald de Grey led the forces that successfully attacked Wales from the north. He was rewarded for his success by being given a castle at Ruthin in north Wales, and the title of the first Lord Grey of Wilton.

In the year 1297 when King Edward went to Flanders leaving his son as the regent in England, he appointed Reginald to be his son's military adviser.

In the same year our former Sheriff was summoned to Parliament, and played a leading role in its development.

Reginald also gave up his role as the Chief Justice of Chester, so that he was free to help King Edward in the many conflicts between England and Scotland.

He had a son named John after his father, who also served his country well, and was to become associated with the Ferrers family when he married Anne, the daughter of William Ferrers.

In the year 1306 we had an instance of the close relationship between King Edward I and Reginald de Grey. Edward wrote off part of a debt which Reginald owed to the King, in consideration of Reginald and his son John's good services to the crown. Edward died in the year 1307 and Reginald was to die shortly after.

Reginald's castle home at Ruthin in north Wales has been preserved and converted into a luxury hotel and in the local churchyard the family graves of the de Grey family can be seen.

After Roger Godberd's release from prison, he lived a quiet and incident free life until his death in the year 1293.

We know he must have died in or around his family home because the post mortem on his death was held in his home county of Leicester.

The geste ballad, which has been a reliable source of information about the outlaws, tells us that when Robin was feeling ill he went to a nearby convent for treatment.

The convent was described as being next to a church, and he went there for the purpose of being let blood. This particular form of treatment was considered in those days and in more modern times to be the cure for most illnesses.

We are told that Robin Hood died at the hands of a relative, and it is very likely therefore that this visit by our outlaw would have been to Garendon Abbey

This Abbey was situated a short distance away from Roger Godberd's home. It had a convent next to the church of the Abbey and because of Roger's family connection to the Abbey it is very probable that a member of Roger's Godberd's family would be associated with the Abbey and working there by tending to the sick.

As mentioned previously Roger leased a portion of his land to the Abbey, which they farmed. His post mortem inquest ruled that Roger's son must carry on the treaty, which the Godberd family had with the Abbey.

This was that the Abbey would continue with their right to part of Roger Godberd's land, which they could cultivate at their pleasure. The transfer of Roger Godberd's estate to his son was also complicated by queries, which had to be settled by a local jury.

This was to determine the rightful ownership of land which the Godberd family had taken in from the wasteland near Charnwood Forest.

They farmed this land and it did of course, increase their landholdings. Another landowner challenged their right to keep this extra land, but the jury ruled in young Roger Godberd's favour that it was lawful for Roger to have taken in this land and cultivated it.

Because of his substantial landowning, young Roger was in later years called upon to serve a knight's service for his country.

Roger Godberd may have died in obscurity after his life as one of England's greatest outlaws, but his struggle for parliamentary reform was achieved after his death.

King Edward I did adopt many of Simon de Montfort's ideas, and moved towards the Parliamentary democracy which we take so much for granted.

There is no public record of the real names of Roger's fellow outlaws, but they certainly existed as the Nottingham authorities and Reginald de Grey knew only too well.

There is a gravestone of Little John that can be seen in the churchyard at Hathersage, a place in Nottingham's neighbouring county of Derbyshire.

The village of Blidworth, which was an important place in Sherwood Forest during Robin Hood's time as an outlaw, claims to have the burial ground of Will Scarlet.

In the original ballads he was known as Will Scarlock and as being a relative of Robin Hood.

Scarlock is a nickname derived from Scarlet meaning red, and lock is an old English term for curly hair. So Will of the red curly hair could well be Roger Godberd's younger brother William who joined Roger at Kenilworth castle and became an important member of the outlaws? Did he settle in Sherwood Forest after his days an outlaw was over?

One of the most popular questions asked about the Robin Hood legend is if Maid Marian really existed. Some writers have rather foolishly doubted her existence because her name doesn't appear in any of the ancient ballads.

Are they saying that Robin Hood never married or had a woman in his life? We know that Roger Godberd was married, and had at least two children, a son named after him, and a daughter named Diva.

Unfortunately at the present time, there is no trace of his wife's name in the public records. It is very likely that at the outlaws base in Perlethorpe members of the outlaws' families would have been present to help their men folk. They were known as camp followers.

We have a similar situation in that the existence of Friar Tuck is in doubt. It is reasonable to assume however that he was a member of the outlaws, knowing the religious feeling of Roger Godberd and the times in which they lived.

Two visitor sites have been built in memory of Robin Hood, one in Nottingham near the castle, and the other at Edwinstowe in the northern part of Sherwood Forest.

The area around Edwinstowe is at the heart of where the outlaws were based, as told by the Geste ballad and public records. We have Perlethorpe the scene of the clash between the outlaws and the authorities near Edwinstowe and the castle home of Richard Foliot at nearby Wellow.

The area is now known as the Dukeries because in the 18th-19th centuries several different Dukes once lived and had estates there.

Perlethorpe is now in the grounds of Thoresby Hall and was used to house the farm workers on the estate, as Roger Godberd would have done to farm and feed his men and their many horses.

The area became known as Robin Hood's meadow.

The historian McCauley recorded the visit of King William 111 to the area as follows;-

'William hunted several times in that forest, the finest in the Kingdom, which in old times gave shelter to Robin Hood and Little John. It is now portioned out into the Lordly domains of Thoresby, Clumber, and Welbeck.'

There is also an old description, written about Robin Hood, which perfectly sums up his life.

'This country has produced no other hero whose popularity has endured so long - While England shall be England, Robin Hood will be a popular name'.